CAMBRIDGE LIBRARY COLLECTION

Books of enduring scholarly value

Archaeology

The discovery of material remains from the recent or the ancient past has always been a source of fascination, but the development of archaeology as an academic discipline which interpreted such finds is relatively recent. It was the work of Winckelmann at Pompeii in the 1760s which first revealed the potential of systematic excavation to scholars and the wider public. Pioneering figures of the nineteenth century such as Schliemann, Layard and Petrie transformed archaeology from a search for ancient artifacts, by means as crude as using gunpowder to break into a tomb, to a science which drew from a wide range of disciplines - ancient languages and literature, geology, chemistry, social history - to increase our understanding of human life and society in the remote past.

Babylonians and Assyrians

Archibald Henry Sayce (1845–1933) became interested in Middle Eastern languages and scripts while still a teenager. Old Persian and Akkadian cuneiform had recently been deciphered, and popular enthusiasm for these discoveries was running high when Sayce began his academic career at Oxford in 1869. This work in 'The Semitic Series', intended to present 'a knowledge of the more important facts' in the history of the Near Eastern civilisations, was published in 1900. Sayce's account begins with the geographical and historical background, and then surveys life in the cities, from the family and its home to the government, the law and the army, economic issues such as slavery, prices and banking, the extent and relevance of literacy, and the importance of religion. Scholarly, but written for a popular audience, this work remains of relevance to anyone interested in studying the everyday lives of ordinary people in this ancient society.

T0372722

Cambridge University Press has long been a pioneer in the reissuing of out-of-print titles from its own backlist, producing digital reprints of books that are still sought after by scholars and students but could not be reprinted economically using traditional technology. The Cambridge Library Collection extends this activity to a wider range of books which are still of importance to researchers and professionals, either for the source material they contain, or as landmarks in the history of their academic discipline.

Drawing from the world-renowned collections in the Cambridge University Library and other partner libraries, and guided by the advice of experts in each subject area, Cambridge University Press is using state-of-the-art scanning machines in its own Printing House to capture the content of each book selected for inclusion. The files are processed to give a consistently clear, crisp image, and the books finished to the high quality standard for which the Press is recognised around the world. The latest print-on-demand technology ensures that the books will remain available indefinitely, and that orders for single or multiple copies can quickly be supplied.

The Cambridge Library Collection brings back to life books of enduring scholarly value (including out-of-copyright works originally issued by other publishers) across a wide range of disciplines in the humanities and social sciences and in science and technology.

Babylonians and Assyrians

Life and Customs

ARCHIBALD HENRY SAYCE

CAMBRIDGE
UNIVERSITY PRESS

CAMBRIDGE
UNIVERSITY PRESS

University Printing House, Cambridge, CB2 8BS, United Kingdom

Cambridge University Press is part of the University of Cambridge.
It furthers the University's mission by disseminating knowledge in the pursuit of
education, learning and research at the highest international levels of excellence.

www.cambridge.org
Information on this title: www.cambridge.org/9781108082365

© in this compilation Cambridge University Press 2018

This edition first published 1900
This digitally printed version 2018

ISBN 978-1-108-08236-5 Paperback

This book reproduces the text of the original edition. The content and language reflect
the beliefs, practices and terminology of their time, and have not been updated.

Cambridge University Press wishes to make clear that the book, unless originally published
by Cambridge, is not being republished by, in association or collaboration with,
or with the endorsement or approval of, the original publisher or its successors in title.

The Semitic Series

BABYLONIANS AND ASSYRIANS

LIFE AND CUSTOMS

REV. A. H. SAYCE

PROFESSOR OF ASSYRIOLOGY AT OXFORD

The Semitic Series

BABYLONIANS AND ASSYRIANS

LIFE AND CUSTOMS

BY THE

REV. A. H. SAYCE

PROFESSOR OF ASSYRIOLOGY AT OXFORD

LONDON

JOHN C. NIMMO

14 KING WILLIAM STREET, STRAND

MDCCCC

A SERIES OF SEMITIC HANDBOOKS

EDITOR'S PREFACE

SEMITIC studies, both linguistically and archæo-logically, have advanced by rapid strides during the last two decades. Fresh light has fallen upon the literary, scientific, theological, mercantile, and other achievements of this great branch of the human family. What these peoples thought and achieved has a very direct bearing upon some of the problems that lie nearest to the hearts of a large portion of the intelligent peoples of Christendom to-day. Classical studies no longer enjoy a monopoly of attention in the curricula of our colleges and universities. It is, in fact, more and more plainly perceived by scholars that among the early peoples who have contributed to the ideas inwrought into our present civilization there is none to whom we owe a greater debt than we do to the Semitic family. Apart from the genetic relation which the thought of these peoples bears to the Christianity of the past and present, a study of their achievements in general has become a matter of

general human interest. It is here that we find the
earliest beginnings of civilization historically known
to us—here that early religious ideas, social customs
and manners, political organizations, the beginnings
of art and architecture, the rise and growth of mytho-
logical ideas that have endured and spread to western nations, can be seen in their earliest stages, and
here alone the information is supplied which enables
us to follow them most successfully in their development.

The object of this series is to present, in brief and
compact form, a knowledge of the more important
facts in the history of this family in a way that will
be serviceable to students in colleges, universities,
and theological seminaries, to the clergy, and to intelligent lay readers.

It has been the good fortune of the Editor and
Publishers to secure the interest and co-operation of
scholars who are fitted by their special knowledge of
the subjects entrusted to them. Works written on
Semitic subjects by those whose knowledge is gained
from other than the original sources are sure to be
defective in many ways. It is only the specialist
whose knowledge enables him to take a comprehen-
sive view of the entire field in which he labors who is
able to gain the perspective necessary for the produc-
tion of a general work which will set forth promi-
nently, and in their proper relations, the salient and
most interesting facts.

Each contributor to the Series presents his contribution subject to no change by the Editor. In cases where it may be deemed of sufficient importance to notice a divergent view this will be done in a foot-note. The authors, however, will aim to make their several contributions consistent with the latest discoveries.

JAMES ALEXANDER CRAIG.

UNIVERSITY OF MICHIGAN,
    September, 1899.

CONTENTS

CHAPTER VIII

CHAPTER IX

CHAPTER X

CHAPTER XI

APPENDIX

BABYLONIANS AND ASSYRIANS

LIFE AND CUSTOMS

BABYLONIAN AND ASSYRIAN LIFE AND CUSTOMS

CHAPTER I

BABYLONIA AND ITS INHABITANTS

BABYLONIA was the gathering-place of the nations. Berossus, the Chaldean historian, tells us that after the creation it was peopled by a mixture of races, and we read in the book of Genesis that Babel, or Babylon, was the first home of the manifold languages of mankind. The country for the most part had been won from the sea; it was the gift of the two great rivers, Euphrates and Tigris, which once flowed separately into the Persian Gulf. Its first settlers must have established themselves on the desert plateau which fringes the Babylonian plain rather than in the plain itself.

The plain is formed of the silt deposited each year by the rivers that flow through it. It is, in fact, as much a delta as Northern Egypt, and is correspondingly fertile. Materials exist for determining approximately the rate at which this delta has been formed. The waters of the Persian Gulf are continually receding from the shore, and Ainsworth[1] cal-

[1] Researches in Assyria, Babylonia, and Chaldea (1838), p. 131 *sqq*.

1

culates that about ninety feet of land are added annually to the coast-line. But the rate of deposit
seems to have been somewhat more rapid in the past.
At all events, Mohammerah, which in 1835 was forty-
seven miles distant from the Gulf, stands on the site
of Spasinus Charax, which, in the time of Alexander
the Great, was not quite a mile from the sea. In
2,160 years, therefore, no less than forty-six miles of
land have been formed at the head of the Persian
Gulf, or nearly one hundred and fifteen feet each
year.

The deposit of soil, however, may not have been so
rapid in the flourishing days of Babylonian history,
when the canals were carefully attended to and the
irrigation of the country kept under control. It is
safer, therefore, to assume for the period preceding
the rise of the Macedonian Empire a rate of deposit
of not more than one hundred feet each year. The
seaport of primitive Chaldea was Eridu, not far from
Ur, and as the mounds of Abu-Shahrein or Nowâwis,
which now mark its site, are nearly one hundred
and thirty miles from the present line of coast, we
must go back as far as 6500 B.C. for the foundation of
the town. "Ur of the Chaldees," as it is called in
the Book of Genesis, was some thirty miles to the
north, and on the same side of the Euphrates ; the
ruins of its great temple of the Moon-god are now
known by the name of Muqayyar or Mugheir. It
must have been founded on the sandy plateau of the
Arabian desert at a time when the plain enclosed
between the Tigris and the Euphrates was still too
marshy for human habitation. As the Moon-god of

Ur was held to be the son of El-lil of Nippur, Dr. Peters is doubtless right in believing that Ur was a colony of the latter city. Nippur is the modern Niffer or Nuffar in the north of Babylonia, and recent excavations have shown that its temple was the chief sanctuary and religious centre of the civilized eastern world in the earliest epoch to which our records reach. Eridu, Ur, and Nippur seem to have been the three chief cities of primeval Babylonia. As we shall see in a future chapter, Eridu and Nippur were the centres from which the early culture and religion of the country were diffused. But there was an essential difference between them. Ea, the god of Eridu, was a god of light and beneficence, who employed his divine wisdom in healing the sick and restoring the dead to life. He had given man all the elements of civilization; rising each morning out of his palace under the waters of the deep, he taught them the arts and sciences, the industries and manners, of civilized life. El-lil of Nippur, on the contrary, was the lord of the underworld; magical spells and incantations were his gifts to mankind, and his kingdom was over the dead rather than the living. The culture which emanated from Eridu and Nippur was thus of a wholly different kind. Is it possible that the settlers in the two cities were of a different race?

Of this there is no proof. Such evidence as we have tells against it. And the contrast in the character of the cultures of Eridu and Nippur can be explained in another way. Eridu was a seaport; its population was in contact with other races, and its

ships traded with the coasts of Arabia. The myth
which told how Ea or Oannes had brought the elements of civilization to his people expressly stated
that he came from the waters of the Persian Gulf.
The culture of Eridu may thus have been due to
foreign intercourse ; Eridu was a city of merchants
and sailors, Nippur of sorcerer-priests.

Eridu and Nippur, however, alike owed their origin to a race which we will term Sumerian.   Its
members spoke agglutinative dialects, and the primitive civilization of Babylonia was their creation.
They were the founders of its great cities and temples, the inventors of the pictorial system of writing
out of which the cuneiform characters subsequently
developed, the instructors in culture of their Semitic
neighbors.   How deep and far-reaching was their
influence may be gathered from the fact that the
earliest civilization of Western Asia finds its expression in the Sumerian language and script.   To whatever race the writer might belong he clothed his
thoughts in the words and characters of the Sumerian people.   The fact makes it often difficult for us
to determine whether the princes of primitive Chaldea whose inscriptions have come down to us were
Semites or not.   Their very names assume Sumerian
forms.

It was from the Sumerian that the Semite learnt
to live in cities.   His own word for " city " was *âlu*,
the Hebrew *'ohel* " a tent," which is still used in the
Old Testament in the sense of "home ;" the Hebrew *'îr* is the Sumerian *eri*. *Ekallu*, the Hebrew
hekal, " a palace," comes from the Sumerian *e-gal* or

"great house;" the first palaces seen by the Semitic nomad must have been those of the Chaldean towns.

But a time came when the Semite had absorbed the culture of his Sumerian teachers and had established kingdoms of his own in the future Babylonia. For untold centuries he lived in intermixture with the older population of the country, and the two races acted and re-acted on each other. A mixed people was the result, with a mixed language and a mixed form of religion. The Babylonia of later days was, in fact, a country whose inhabitants and language were as composite as the inhabitants and language of modern England. Members of the same family had names derived from different families of speech, and while the old Sumerian borrowed Semitic words which it spelt phonetically, the Semitic lexicon was enriched with loan-words from Sumerian which were treated like Semitic roots.

The Semite improved upon the heritage he had received. Even the system of writing was enlarged and modified. Its completion and arrangement are due to Semitic scribes who had been trained in Sumerian literature. It was probably at the court of Sargon of Akkad that what we may term the final revision of the syllabary took place. At all events, after his epoch the cuneiform script underwent but little real change.

Sargon was the founder of the first Semitic empire in Asia. His date was placed by the native historians as far back as 3800 B.C., and as they had an abundance of materials at their disposal for settling it, which we do not possess, we have no reason to

dispute it. Moreover, it harmonizes with the length
of time required for bringing about that fusion of
Sumerian and Semitic elements which created the
Babylonia we know. The power of Sargon extended
to the Mediterranean, even, it may be, to the island
of Cyprus. His conquests were continued by his
son and successor Naram-Sin, who made his way to
the precious copper-mines of the Sinaitic peninsula,
the chief source of the copper that was used so
largely in the work of his day. "The land of the
Amorites," as Syria was called, was already a Babylonian province, and he could therefore march in
safety toward the south through the desert region
which was known as Melukhkha.

How long the empire of Sargon lasted we do not
know. But it spread Babylonian culture to the distant west and brought it to the very border of Egypt.
It was, too, a culture which had become essentially
Semitic; the Sumerian elements on which it was
based had been thoroughly transformed. What
Babylonian civilization was in the latest days of
Chaldean history, that it already was, to all intents
and purposes, in the age of Sargon. The Sumerian
and the Semite had become one people.

But the mixture of nationalities in Babylonia was
not yet complete. Colonies of Amorites, from Canaan,
settled in it for the purposes of trade; wandering
tribes of Semites, from Northern Arabia, pastured
their cattle on the banks of its rivers, and in the
Abrahamic age a line of kings from Southern Arabia
made themselves masters of the country, and established their capital at Babylon. Their names re-

sembled those of Southern Arabia on the one hand, of the Hebrews on the other, and the Babylonian scribes were forced to give translations of them in their own language.

But all these incomers belonged to the Semitic race, and the languages they spoke were but varieties of the same family of speech. It is probable that such was the case with the Kaldâ, who lived in the marshes at the mouth of the Euphrates, and from whom classical geography has derived the name of Chaldean. The extension of the name to the whole population of Babylonia was due to the reign of the Kaldâ prince, Merodach-baladan, at Babylon. For years he represented Babylonian freedom in its struggle with Assyria, and his "Chaldean" subjects became an integral part of the population. Perhaps, too, the theory is right which makes Nebuchadnezzar of Kaldâ descent. If so, there is a good reason why the inhabitants of Babylonia should have become "Chaldeans" in the classical age.

Of wholly different origin were the Kassites, mountaineers from the east of Elam, who conquered Babylonia, and founded a dynasty of kings which lasted for several centuries. They also gave their name to the population of the country, and, in the Tel-el-Amarna tablets, accordingly, the natives of Babylonia are known as " Kassi." Sennacherib found their kinsfolk in the Elamite mountains, and here they still lived in the age of the Greek writers. Strabo calls them Kosseans, and it seems probable that they are the same as the Kissians, after whom the whole of Elam was named. At any rate the Kassites were neither Sumerians nor Semites; and their language, of which several words have been preserved, has no known connections. But they left their mark upon the Babylonian people, and several family names were borrowed from them.

The Babylonian was thus a compound of Sumerian, Semitic, and Kassite elements. They all went to form the culture which we term Babylonian, and which left such enduring traces on Western Asia and the world. Mixed races are invariably the best, and the Babylonians were no exception to the rule. We have only to compare them with their neighbors, the more purely blooded Semitic Assyrians, to assure ourselves of the fact. The culture of Assyria was but an imitation and reflection of that of Babylonia— there was nothing original about it. The Assyrian excelled only in the ferocities of war, not in the arts of peace. Even the gods of Assyria had migrated from the southern kingdom.

The dual character of Babylonian civilization must never be forgotten. It serves to explain a good deal that would otherwise be puzzling in the religious and social life of the people. But the social life was also influenced and conditioned by the peculiar nature of the country in which the people lived. It was an alluvial plain, sloping toward the sea, and inundated by the overflow of the two great rivers which ran through it. When cultivated it was exceedingly fertile; but cultivation implied a careful regulation of the overflow, as well as a constant attention to the embankments which kept out the waters, or to the canals which drained and watered the soil.

The inhabitants were therefore, necessarily, agriculturists. They were also irrigators and engineers, compelled to study how best to regulate the supply of water, to turn the pestiferous marsh into a fruitful field, and to confine the rivers and canals within their channels. Agriculture and engineering thus had their natural home in Babylonia, and originated in the character of the country itself.

The neighborhood of the sea and the two great waterways which flanked the Babylonian plain further gave an impetus to trade. The one opened the road to the spice-bearing coasts of Southern Arabia and the more distant shores of Egypt; the other led to the highlands of Western Asia. From the first the Babylonians were merchants and sailors as well as agriculturists. The "cry" of the Chaldeans was "in their ships." The seaport of Eridu was one of the earliest of Babylonian cities; and a special form of boat took its name from the more inland town of Ur. While the population of the country devoted itself to agriculture, the towns grew wealthy by the help of trade.

Their architecture was dependent on the nature of the country. In the alluvial plain no stone was procurable; clay, on the other hand, was everywhere. All buildings, accordingly, were constructed of clay bricks, baked in the sun, and bonded together with cement of the same material; their roofs were of wood, supported, not unfrequently, by the stems of the palm. The palm stems, in time, became pillars, and Babylonia was thus the birthplace of columnar architecture. It was also the birthplace of decorated

walls. It was needful to cover the sun-dried bricks
with plaster, for the sake both of their preservation
and of appearance. This was the origin of the stucco
with which the walls were overlaid, and which came
in time to be ornamented with painting. Ezekiel
refers to the figures, portrayed in vermilion, which
adorned the walls of the houses of the rich.

The want of stone and the abundance of clay had
another and unique influence upon Babylonian culture. It led to the invention of the written clay tablet, which has had such momentous results for the
civilization of the whole Eastern world. The pictures
with which Babylonian writing began were soon discarded for the conventional forms, which could so
easily be impressed by the stylus upon the soft clay.
It is probable that the use of the clay as a writing
material was first suggested by the need there was
in matters of business that the contracting parties
should record their names. The absence of stone
made every pebble valuable, and pebbles were accordingly cut into cylindrical forms and engraved with
signs. When the cylinder was rolled over a lump of
wet clay, its impress remained forever. The signs
became cuneiform characters, and the Babylonian
wrote them upon clay instead of stone.

The seal-cylinder and the use of clay as a writing
material must consequently be traced to the peculiar
character of the country in which the Babylonian
lived. To the same origin must be ascribed his
mode of burial. The tomb was built of bricks ;
there were no rocky cliffs in which to excavate it, and
the marshy soil made a grave unsanitary. It was

doubtless sanitary reasons alone that caused wood to be heaped about the tomb after an interment and set on fire so that all within it was partially consumed. The narrow limits of the Babylonian plain obliged the cemetery of the dead to adjoin the houses of the living, and cremation, whether partial or complete, became a necessity.

Even the cosmogony of the Babylonians has been influenced by their surroundings. The world, it was believed, originated in a watery chaos, like that in which the first settlers had found the Babylonian plain. The earth not only rested on the waters, but the waters themselves, dark and unregulated, were the beginning of all things. This cosmological conception was carried with the rest of Babylonian culture to the West, and after passing through Canaan found its way into Greek philosophy. In the Book of Genesis we read that "darkness was on the face of the deep" before the creative spirit of God brooded over it, and Thales, the first of Greek philosophers, taught that water was the principle out of which all things have come.

The fertility of the Babylonian soil was remarkable. Grain, it was said, gave a return of two hundred for one, sometimes of three hundred for one. Herodotus, or the authority he quotes, grows enthusiastic upon the subject. "The leaf of the wheat and barley," he says, "is as much as three inches in width, and the stalks of the millet and sesamum are so tall that no one who has never been in that country would believe me were I to mention their height." In fact, naturalists tell us that Babylonia was the primitive home of the cultivated cereals, wheat and probably barley, and that from the banks of the Euphrates they must have been disseminated throughout the civilized world. Wheat, indeed, has been found growing wild in our own days in the neighborhood of Hit.

The dissemination of wheat goes back to a remote epoch. Like barley, it is met with in the tombs of that prehistoric population of Egypt which still lived in the neolithic age and whose later remains are coeval with the first Pharaonic epoch. The fact throws light on the antiquity of the intercourse which existed between the Euphrates and the Nile, and bears testimony to the influence already exerted on the Western world by the culture of Babylonia. We have, indeed, no written records which go back to so distant a past; it belongs, perhaps, to an epoch when the art of writing had not as yet been invented. But there was already civilization in Babylonia, and the elements of its future social life were already in existence. Babylonian culture is immeasurably old.

CHAPTER II

THE FAMILY

Two principles struggled for recognition in Babylonian family life. One was the patriarchal, the other the matriarchal. Perhaps they were due to a duality of race; perhaps they were merely a result of the circumstances under which the Babylonian lived. At times it would seem as if we must pronounce the Babylonian family to have been patriarchal in its character; at other times the wife and mother occupies an independent and even commanding position. It may be noted that whereas in the old Sumerian hymns the woman takes precedence of the man, the Semitic translation invariably reverses the order: the one has "female and male," the other "male and female." Elsewhere in the Semitic world, where the conceptions of Babylonian culture had not penetrated, the woman was subordinate to the man, his helpmate and not his equal.

In this respect nothing can be more significant than the changes undergone by the name and worship of the goddess Istar, when they were carried from Babylonia to the Semites of the West. In Babylonia she was a goddess of independent power, who stood on a footing of equality with the gods. But in

13

Southern Arabia and Moab she became a male
divinity, and in the latter country was even identified with the supreme god Chemosh. In Canaan she
passed into the feminine Ashtoreth, and at last was
merged in the crowd of goddesses who were but the
feminine reflections of the male. A goddess whose
attributes did not differ from those of a god was
foreign to the religious ideas of the purely Semitic
mind.

It was otherwise in Babylonia. There the goddess
was the equal of the god, while on earth the women
claimed rights which placed them almost on a level
with the men. One of the early sovereigns of the
country was a queen, Ellat-Gula, and even in Assyria
the bas-reliefs of Assur-bani-pal represent the queen
as sitting and feasting by the side of her husband.
A list of trees brought to Akkad in the reign of Sargon
(3800 B.C.) speaks of them as having been conveyed
by the servants of the queen, and if Dr. Scheil is
right in his translation of the Sumerian words, the
kings of Ur, before the days of Abraham, made their
daughters high-priestesses of foreign lands.

Up to the last the Babylonian woman, in her
own name, could enter into partnership with others,
could buy and sell, lend and borrow, could appear
as plaintiff and witness in a court of law, could
even bequeath her property as she wished. In a
deed, dated in the second year of Nabonidos (555
B.C.), a father transfers all his property to his daughter, reserving to himself only the use of it during
the rest of his life. In return the daughter agrees
to provide him with the necessaries of life, food and

drink, oil and clothing. A few years later, in the
second year of Cyrus, a woman of the name of
Nubta, or "Bee," hired out a slave for five years in
order that he might be taught the art of weaving.
She stipulated to give him one *qa*, or about a quart
and a half of food, each day, and to provide him with
clothing while he was learning the trade. It is
evident that Nubtâ owned looms and traded in woven
fabrics on her own account.

Nubta was the daughter of Ben-Hadad-amara, a
Syrian *settled* in Babylonia who had been adopted
by another Syrian of the name of Ben-Hadad-nathan.
After the latter's death his widow brought an action
before the royal judges to recover her husband's
property. She stated that after their marriage she
and Ben-Hadad-nathan had traded together, and that
a house had been purchased with a portion of her
dowry. This house, the value of which was as much
as 110 manehs, 50 shekels, or £62 10s., had been
assigned to her in perpetuity. The half-brother
Aqabi-il (Jacob-el), however, now claimed everything,
including the house. The case was tried at Babylon
before six judges in the ninth year of Nabonidos,
and they decided in favor of the plaintiff.

One of the documents that have come down to us
from the age of Abraham records the gift of a female
slave by a husband to his wife. The slave and her
children, it was laid down, were to remain the property of the wife in case either of divorce or of the
husband's death. The right of the woman to hold
private property of her own, over which the male
heirs had no control, was thus early recognized by

the law. In later times it is referred to in number-
less contracts. In the reign of Nebokin-abla, for
instance, in the eleventh century B.C., we find a field
bequeathed first of all to a daughter and then to a
sister; in the beginning of the reign of Nabonidos
we hear of a brother and sister, the children of a
naturalized Egyptian, inheriting their father's property together; and in the fourth year of Cyrus his
son Cambyses sued for the payment of a loan which
he had made to a Babylonian on the security of some
house-property, and which was accordingly refunded
by the debtor's wife.   Other deeds relate to the
borrowing of money by a husband and his wife in
partnership, to a wife selling a slave for a maneh of
silver on her own account, to a woman bringing
an action before six judges at the beginning of the
reign of Nabonidos to recover the price of a slave
she had sold, and to another woman who two years
previously was the witness to the sale of a house.
Further proofs are not needed of the independent
position of the woman, whether married or single,
and of her equality with the man in the eyes of the
law.

It would seem that she was on a level with him
also in the eyes of religion. There were priestesses
in Babylonia as well as priests. The oracles of Istar
at Arbela were worked by inspired prophetesses, who
thus resembled Deborah and Huldah and the other
prophetesses of Israel. When Esar-haddon inquired
of the will of heaven, it was from the prophetesses of
Istar that he received encouragement and a promise
of victory. From the earliest period, moreover, there

were women who lived like nuns, unmarried and devoted to the service of the Sun-god. The office was held in high honor, one of the daughters of King Ammi-Zadok, the fourth successor of Khammurabi or Amraphel, being a devotee of the god. In the reign of the same king we find two of these devotees and their nieces letting for a year nine feddans or acres of ground in the district in which the "Amorites" of Canaan were settled. This was done "by command of the high-priest Sar-ilu," a name in which Mr. Pinches suggests that we should see that of Israel. The women were to receive a shekel of silver, or three shillings, "the produce of the field," by way of rent, while six measures of corn on every ten feddans were to be set apart for the Sun-god himself. In the previous reign a house had been let at an annual rent of two shekels which was the joint property of a devotee of the Sun-god Samas and her brother. It is clear that consecration to the service of the deity did not prevent the "nun" from owning and enjoying property.

Like Samas, the Sun-god, Istar was also served by women, who, however, do not seem to have led the same reputable lives. They were divided into two classes, one of which was called the "Wailers," from the lamentations with which each year they mourned the death of the god Tammuz, the stricken favorite of Istar. The Chaldean Epic of Gilgames speaks of the "troops" of them that were gathered together in the city of Erech. Here Istar had her temple along with her father, Anu, the Sky-god, and here accordingly her devotees were assembled. Like the goddess they

served, it would appear that they were never married
in lawful wedlock. But they nevertheless formed a
corporation, like the corporations of the priests.

Babylonian law and custom prevailed also in Assyria. So far as can be gathered from the contracts
that have come down to us, the Assyrian women enjoyed almost as many privileges as their sisters in
Babylonia. Thus, in 668 B.C., we find a lady, Tsarpî
by name, buying the sister of a man whose slave she
was, for reasons unknown to us, and paying half a
maneh of silver (£4 10s.) for the girl. Tsarpî was a
"prefectess," like another lady who is called "the
prefectess of Nineveh," and who, in 683 B.C., purchased seventeen slaves and a garden. It is plain
from this that women could hold civil offices and even
act as governors of a city.

In fact, wherever Babylonian culture and law extended, the principles and practice of it were necessarily in force. The Amorite colonies from Canaan established in Babylonia for the purposes of trade in the
age of Abraham were naturally subject to the Babylonian laws, and the women among them possessed
all the rights of their Babylonian neighbors. At the
very beginning of the dynasty to which Khammurabi
belonged, an Amorite lady, a certain Kuryatum,
brought an action for the recovery of a field which
had been the property of her father, Asalia, and won
her suit. Kuryatum and her brother were themselves
subsequently sued by three other "Amorites," the
children of Izi-idrê, one of whom was a woman, for
a field and house, together with some slaves and palm-
trees, of which, it was asserted, they had wrongfully

taken possession. The judges, however, after hearing both sides, dismissed the case.

It is not strange that the same laws and principles should have held good in Canaan itself, which was so long a Babylonian province. Sarah, who was of Babylonian origin, owned a female slave (Gen. xvi. 2, 6, 8, 9), and the Kennizzite Caleb assigned a field with springs to his daughter Achsah in the early days of the invasion of Canaan (Josh. xv. 18, 19). A Canaanitish lady takes part in the Tel-el-Amarna correspondence, and writes to the Pharaoh on matters of state, while the Mosaic Law allowed the daughter to inherit the possessions of her father (Numb. xxxvi. 8). This, however, was only the case where there was no son; after the Israelitish conquest of Canaan, when the traditions of Babylonian custom had passed away, we hear no more of brothers and sisters sharing together the inheritance of their father, or of a wife bequeathing anything which belongs to her of right. As regards the woman, the law of Israel, after the settlement in Canaan, was the moral law of the Semitic tribes. We must go back to the age of Abraham and Sarah to find a Hebrew woman possessed of the same powers as the Babylonian lady who, in the fifth year of Cambyses, sold a slave for two manehs and five shekels of silver, her husband and mother guaranteeing the value of the chattel that was thus sold.

The dowry which the woman brought with her on marriage secured of itself her independence. It was her absolute property, and she could leave it by will as she pleased. It protected her from tyrannical con-

duct on the part of her husband, as well as from the
fear of divorce on insufficient grounds. If a divorce
took place the dowry had to be restored to her in full,
and she then returned to her father's house or set up
an establishment of her own. Where no dowry had
been brought by the bride, the husband was often required by the marriage contract to pay her a specified
sum of money in case of her divorce. Thus a marriage contract made in Babylon in the thirteenth
year of Nebuchadnezzar stipulates that, if the husband
marries a second wife, the act shall be equivalent to
a divorce of the first wife, who shall accordingly receive not only her dowry, but a maneh of silver as
well. The payment, in fact, was a penalty on the
unfaithfulness of the husband and served as a check
upon both divorce and polygamy.

The dowry consisted not of money alone, but also
of slaves and furniture, the value of which was stated
in the marriage contract. In the contract just referred to, for instance, part of the dowry consisted of
a slave who was valued at half a maneh. Sometimes
the dowry included cattle and sheep. In the sixth
year of Nabonidos we hear of three slaves and " furniture with which to stock the house," besides a maneh
of silver (£6), being given as the marriage-portion.
In this instance, however, the silver was not forthcoming on the wedding-day, and in place of it a slave
valued at two-thirds of a maneh was accepted, the remaining third being left for payment at a subsequent
date. Where the dowry could not be paid at once,
security for the payment of it was taken by the
bridegroom.

The payment was made, not by the bridegroom, as among the Israelites and other Semitic peoples, but by the father of the bride. If he were dead, or if the mother of the bride had been divorced and was in the enjoyment of her own property, the mother took the place of the father and was expected to provide the dowry. In such a case she also naturally gave permission for the marriage, and it was from her accordingly that consent to it had to be obtained. In one instance, however, in a deed dated in the sixteenth year of Nabonidos, a sister is given in marriage by her two brothers, who consequently furnish the dowry, consisting of a piece of ground inherited from the mother, a slave, clothes, and furniture. It is evident that in this case both the parents must have been dead.

It was the bridegroom's duty and interest to see that the dowry was duly paid. He enjoyed the usufruct of it during his life, and not unfrequently it was employed not only to furnish the house of the newly married couple, but also to start them in business. It was with his wife's dowry that Ben-Hadad-nathan bought in part the house to which his widow laid claim after his death, and we read of instances in which the husband and wife enter into partnership in order to trade with the wife's money. More frequently the wife uses her dowry to transact business separately, her purchases and loans being made in her own name; this is especially the case if she otherwise has property of her own.[1]

---

[1] In certain cases the wife seems to have had the power of claiming alimony from her husband, though we do not know what were the circumstances which were held sufficient to justify the claim.

At times the son-in-law found it difficult to get the dowry paid. From a deed dated in the third year of Cambyses we gather that the dowry, instead of being delivered "into the hand" of the bridegroom, as ought to have been done at the time of the marriage, was still unpaid nine years later. Sometimes, of course, this was due to the inability of the father-in-law to discharge his debt, through bankruptcy, death, or other causes. Where, therefore, the money was not immediately forthcoming, security was taken for its future payment. If payment in full was impossible, owing to pecuniary losses incurred after the marriage contract had been drawn up, the bridegroom was entitled to claim a proportionate amount of it on behalf of his wife. The heirs were called upon to pay what was due if the father-in-law died between the drawing-up of the contract and the actual marriage, and when the wife died without children it returned to her "father's house."

If the husband died and his widow married again, she carried her former dowry with her. In such a case the children of the first marriage inherited two-thirds of it upon her death, the remaining third going to the children of the second husband. This was in accordance with a law which regulated the succession

---

Thus, in the third year of Nabonidos, ' Nahid-Merodach, the son of Samas-baladhu-iqbi, voluntarily granted his wife Ramûa and his son Arad-Bunene four *qas* of food and three *qas* of beer daily, as well as fifteen manehs of wool, one *pi* of sesame, one *pi* of salt, and sixty *qas* of sweetmeats each year," with the provision that the grant should never be cancelled or willed away. The son, however, is included in the gift, and it is possible, therefore, that Ramûa was little more than a concubine.

to the property of a father who had married a second time, the children of the first marriage receiving two-thirds of it and the remainder being reserved for the children of the second wife. The law could only be overruled by a will made during the man's lifetime, and properly attested by witnesses.

The dowry could not be alienated by the wife without the consent of her parents, if they were still alive. In the year of Nergal-sharezer's accession, for example, a certain Nergal-ballidh and his wife Dhib-tá wished to sell a slave, who had constituted the dowry of Dhibta, for twenty-five shekels, but the sale was not considered valid until the consent of both her father and mother had been obtained.

The dowry was not the only property the woman was able to hold. She had similar power to hold and dispose of whatever else had come to her by inheritance or gift. The gains she made in business, the proceeds of the sale of her estates, and the interest upon the capital she lent, all belonged to herself, and to herself alone. For purposes of succession they were reckoned along with the dowry as constituting her property during life. In the thirty-fourth year of Nebuchadnezzar, for instance, a father stipulates that the creditors of his daughter's father-in-law should have no claim either upon her dowry or upon any other part of her possessions.

The power of the married woman over her property was doubtless the result of the system which provided her with a dowry. The principle of her absolute control over the latter once admitted, it was extended by the law to the rest of her estate. She thus

took rank by the side of the man, and, like him, could
trade or otherwise deal with her property as she
chose. The dowry, in fact, must have been her original charter of freedom.

But it was so because it was given by her father,
and not by the bridegroom. Where it was the gift of
the bridegroom it was but a civilized form of purchasing the bride. In such a case the husband had a
right to the person and possessions of the wife, inas-
much as he had bought her ; as much right, in fact, as
he had to the person and possessions of a slave. The
wife was merely a superior slave.

Where, however, the dowry was the gift of the
bride's father the conditions were reversed. The
husband received not only a wife, he received also an
estate along with her. He it was upon whom the
benefit was conferred, and he had to accept the conditions offered him, not to make them. In a commercial state like Babylonia, property represented
personalty, and the personalty of the wife accordingly remained with the family from which her property was derived, rather than with the husband, to
whom the use of it was lent. Hence the independence of the married woman in Babylonia and her
complete freedom of action as regards her husband.
The property she possessed, the personalty it represented, belonged to herself alone.

Traces, however, may be detected of an older order
of things, which once existed, at all events, in the
Semitic element of the Babylonian population. The
dowry had to be paid to the husband, to be deposited, as it were, in his " hand." It was with him that

the marriage contract was made. This must surely
go back to an age when the marriage portion was
really given to the bridegroom, and he had the same
right over it as was enjoyed until recently by the
husband in England. Moreover, the right of divorce
retained by the husband, like the fact that the bride
was given away by a male relation, points in the same
direction. According to an early Sumerian law, while
the repudiation of the wife on the part of the husband was punishable only with a small fine, for the
repudiation of the husband by the wife the penalty
was death. A deed drawn up in the time of Khammurabi shows that this law was still in force in the
age of Abraham. It lays down that if the wife is
unfaithful to her husband she may be drowned, while
the husband can rid himself of his wife by the payment only of a maneh of silver. Indeed, as late as
the time of Nebuchadnezzar, the old law remained
unrepealed, and we find a certain Nebo-akhi-iddin,
who married a singing-woman, stipulating in the
marriage contract that if he should divorce her and
marry another he was to pay her six manehs, but if,
on the contrary, she committed adultery, she should
be put to death with "an iron sword."

In this instance, however, the husband married
beneath him, and in view of the antecedents of the
wife the penalty with which she was threatened in
case of unfaithfulness was perhaps necessary. She
came to him, moreover, without either a dowry or
family relations who could give her away. She was
thus little better than the concubines whom the
Babylonian was allowed to keep by the side of his

lawful wife. But even so, the marriage contract had
to be made out in full legal form, and the penalty to
be paid for her divorce was as much as £54. With
this she could have lived comfortably and probably
have had no difficulty in finding another husband.

The concubine was usually a slave who had been
bought by the bridegroom. Occasionally, by agreement with the parents, the wife herself was in much
the same position. Thus Dagil-ili, who married the
daughter of a lady named Khammâ, gave the mother
one and a half manehs of silver and a slave worth
half a maneh, and agreed that if he married another
wife he would give her daughter a maneh and send
her back to her old home. Here the husband practically buys his wife, though even so the law obliged
him to divorce her if he married again, and also fined
him for doing so. Khamma was apparently in finan-
cial difficulties, and consequently, instead of furnish-
ing her daughter with a dowry, received money from
the bridegroom. It was a private arrangement, and
utterly opposed to the usual custom. The parents
had, however, the power of selling their children
before they came of age, and where the parents were
dead, the same power was possessed—at any rate in
Assyria—by a brother in the case of a sister. Doubtless the power was restricted by law, but the instances
in which we hear of its being exercised are so rare
that we do not know what these restrictions were.

Nor do we know the reasons which were considered
sufficient to justify divorce. The language of the
early laws would seem to imply that originally it was
quite enough to pronounce the words : "Thou art not

my wife," " Thou art not my husband." But the loss
of the wife's dowry and the penalties attached to
divorce must have tended to check it on the part of
the husband, except in exceptional circumstances.
Perhaps want of children was held to be a sufficient
pretext for it ; certainly adultery must have been so.
Another cause of divorce was a legal one : a second
marriage invalidated the first, if the first wife was still
alive.

This is a very astonishing fact in a country where
polygamy was allowed. It proves that polygamy was
greatly restricted in practice, and that the tendency
of the law was to forbid it altogether. Among the
multitudinous contracts of the second Babylonian empire it is difficult to find any which show that a man
had two legitimate wives living at one and the same
time. The high position of the mother of the family,
her independence and commercial equality with her
husband, were all against it. It is only where the
wife is a bought slave that polygamy can flourish.

In early times, it is true, the rich Babylonian in-
dulged in the possession of more than one wife.
Some contracts of the age of Khammurabi, translated
by Mr. Pinches, are particularly instructive in this
respect. We hear in them of a certain Arad-Samas,
who first married a lady called Taram-Sagila and
then her adopted sister Iltani. Iltani, it is ordained,
shall be under the orders of her sister, shall prepare
her food, carry her chair to the Temple of Merodach,
and obey her in all things. Not a word is said about
the divorce of the first wife; it is taken for granted
that she is to remain at the head of the household,

the younger and second wife acting as her servant.
The position of Iltani, in fact, is not very different
from that of a slave, and it is significant that neither
wife brought a dowry with her.

As we have seen in the case of Dagil-ili, the law
and custom of later Babylonia display a complete
change of feeling and practice. Marriage with a
second wife came to involve, as a matter of course,
divorce from the first, even where there had been a
mesalliance and the first wife had been without a
dowry. The woman had thus gained a second victory; the rule that bound her in regard to marriage
was now applied to the man. The privilege of mar-
rying two husbands at once had been denied her;
usage was now denying a similar privilege to him.
It was only when the first wife was dead or divorced
that a second could be taken; the wife might have a
successor, but not a rival.

The divorced wife was regarded by the law as a
widow, and could therefore marry again. A deed of
divorce, dated in the reign of the father of Khammurabi, expressly grants her this right. To the re-
marriage of the widow there was naturally no bar;
but the children by the two marriages belonged to
different families, and were kept carefully distinct.
This is illustrated by a curious deed drawn up at
Babylon, in the ninth year of Nabonidos. A certain Bel-Katsir, who had been adopted by his uncle,
married a widow who already had a son. She bore
him no children, however, and he accordingly asked
the permission of his uncle to adopt his step-son,
thereby making him the heir of his uncle's property.

To this the uncle objected, and it was finally agreed that if Bel-Katsir had no child he was to adopt his own brother, and so secure the succession of the estate to a member of his own family. The property of the mother probably went to her son ; but she had the power to leave it as she liked. This may be gathered from a will, dated in the seventh year of Cyrus, in which a son leaves property to his father in case of death, which had come to him from his maternal grandfather and grandmother. The property had been specially bequeathed to him, doubtless after his mother's death, the grandmother passing over the rest of her descendants in his favor.

The marriage ceremony was partly religious, partly civil; no marriage was legally valid without a contract duly attested and signed. The Babylonians carried their business habits into all departments of life, and in the eyes of the law matrimony was a legal contract, the forms of which had to be duly observed. In the later days of Babylonian history the legal and civil aspect of the rite seems to have been exclusively considered, but at an earlier period it required also the sanction of religion ; and Mr. Pinches has published a fragmentary Sumerian text in which the religious ceremony is described. Those who officiated at it, first placed their hands and feet against the hands and feet of the bridegroom, then the bride laid her neck by the side of his, and he was made to say to her: "Silver and gold shall fill thy lap ; thou art my wife ; I am thy husband. Like the fruit of an orchard will I give thee offspring." Next came the ceremony of binding the sandals on the feet of the newly wedded pair and of handing them the latchet wherewith the shoes should be tied, as well as "a purse of silver and gold." The purse perhaps symbolized the dowry, which was given by the father of the bride. In the time of Nebuchadnezzar the ceremony was restricted to joining together the hands of the bride and bridegroom.

Contact with the Assyrians and Babylonians in the Exilic period introduced the Babylonian conception of the legal character of marriage among the Israelites, and, contrary to the older custom, it became necessary that it should be attested by a written contract. Thus, Raguel, when he gave his daughter "to be wife to Tobias," "called Edna, his wife, and took paper and did write an instrument of covenants, and sealed it " (Tobit vii. 14).

According to Herodotus, a gigantic system of public prostitution prevailed in Babylonia. Every unmarried woman was compelled to remain in the sacred enclosure of Mylitta—by which Istar is apparently meant—until some stranger had submitted to her embraces, while the sums derived from the sale of their personal charms by the handsome and goodlooking provided portions for the ugly. Of all this there is not a trace in the mass of native documents which we now possess. There were the devotees of Istar, certainly—the *ukhâtu* and *kharimâtu*—as well as public prostitutes, who were under the protection of the law; but they formed a class apart, and had nothing to do with the respectable women of the country. On the contrary, in the age of Khammurabi it was customary to state in the marriage contracts that no stain whatever rested on the bride. Thus we read in one of them: "Ana-Â-uzni is the daughter of Salimat. Salimat has given her a dowry, and has offered her in marriage to Bel-sunu, the son of the artisan. Ana-Â-uzni is pure; no one has anything against her." The dowry, as we have seen, was paid by the near relations of the wife, and where there was none, as in the case of the singing-woman married by Nebo-akhi-iddin, there was no dowry at all. The dowries provided for the ugly by the prostitution of the rich must be an invention of the Greeks.

Within what degree of relationship marriage was permitted is uncertain. A man could marry his sister-in-law, as among the Israelites, and, in one instance, we hear of marriage with a niece. In the time of Cambyses a brother marries his half-sister by the same father; but this was probably an imitation of the Persian custom.

The children, as we have seen, whether boys or girls, inherited alike, subject to the provisions of the parent's will. The will seems to have been of Babylonian origin. Testamentary devolution of property went back to an early period in a country in which the legal relations of trade had been so fully developed. Trade implied private property and the idea of individual possession. The estate belonging to a person was his absolutely, to deal with pretty much as he would. He had the same right to alienate it as he had to increase it. In a commercial community there could be no community of goods.

As far back, therefore, as our materials carry us, the unit in the Babylonian state is the individual

rather than the family. It is he with whom both
the law and the government deal, and the legal code
of Babylonia is based upon the doctrine of individual
responsibility. Private ownership is the key-note of
Babylonian social life.

But the whole of this social life was fenced about
by a written law. No title was valid for which a
written document could not be produced, drawn up
and attested in legal forms. The extensive commercial transactions of the Babylonians made this
necessary, and the commercial spirit dominated
Babylonian society. The scribe and the lawyer were
needed at almost every juncture of life.

The invention of the will, or documentary testament, followed naturally. The same legal powers
that were required to protect a man's property during his lifetime were even more urgently required
when he was dead. The will was at first the title
which gave the heir his father's estate. Gradually it
developed, until at last it came to be an instrument
by means of which the testator retained control over
his property even after his death. As an example of
the form which it usually assumed, we may take one
which was drawn up in the seventh year of the reign
of Cyrus as King of Babylon (532 B. C.):

Nebo-baladan, the son of Samas-palassar, the son of the
priest of the Sun-god, has, of his own free-will, sealed all his
estate, which he had inherited from Nebo-balasu-iqbi, the son
of Nur-Ea, the son of the priest of the Sun-god, the father of
his mother, and from Kabtâ, the mother of Assat-Belit, his
grandmother, consisting of a piece of land, a house and the
slaves or serfs attached to it, in accordance with the will (*liter-*

ally tablet) which his maternal grandfather, Nebo-balasu-iqbi, and his maternal grandmother, Kabtâ, had sealed and bequeathed to Nebo-baladan, the son of their daughter, and has bequeathed them for ever to Samas-palassar, the son of Samas-ina-esi-edher, the son of the priest of the Sun-god. As long as Nebo-baladan lives the piece of ground, the house, the slaves, and all the rest of his property shall continue in his own possession, according to the terms of this his will. Whoever shall attempt to change them, may Anu, Bel, and Ae curse him; may Nebo, the divine scribe of E-Saggil, cut off his days! This will has been sealed in the presence of Sula, son of Bania, son of Epes-ilu; of Bel-iddin, son of Bel-natsir, son of the priest of Gula; of Nebo-sum-yukin, son of Sula, son of Sigua; of Nebo-natsir, son of Ziria, son of Sumâti . . .; of Nebo-sum-lisir, son of Nebo-sum-iskun, son of the wine-merchant (?), and the scribe Samas-zir-yusabsi, son of Zariqu-iddin, son of the architect. (Written at) Babylon, the 19th day of Sebat (February), the seventh year of Cyrus, king of Babylon and the world.

In this case it is a son who makes over his property to his father should he be the first to die. The will shows that the son was absolute master of his own possessions even during his father's lifetime, and could bequeath it as he chose.

A remarkable instance of the application of the principles underlying testamentary devolution is to be found in the case of Ninip-Sum-iskun, the son of a land-surveyor who handed over his property to his daughter Dhabtu, while he was still alive, stipulating only for the usufruct of it. The text begins by saying that the testator called to his daughter: "Bring me writing materials, for I am ill. My brother has deserted me; my son has offended me. To you therefore I turn. Have pity on me, and while I live support me with food, oil, and clothes. The income from my surveying business, in which I have two-thirds of a share with my brother, do I hand over to you." After this preamble the deed is drawn up in due form, attested, dated, and sealed. The whole of the testator's property is assigned to his daughter " for ever," " the usufruct of his income " only being reserved to himself "as long as he shall live." He undertakes accordingly not to "sell " it, not to give it to another, not to pawn it or alienate a portion of it. By way of doubly securing that the deed shall take effect, the gods are invoked as well as the law.[1]

---

[1] A similar case, in which, however, it is a testatrix who hands over her property to her son during her lifetime, is recorded in a deed dated at Babylon the 10th day of Sivân, in the second year of Nabonidos. The deed is as follows: " Gugûa, the daughter of Zakir, the son of a native of Isin, has voluntarily sealed and delivered to her eldest son, Ea-zir-ibni, her dowry, consisting of one maneh which is in the keeping of Nebo-akhi-iddin, the son of Sula, the son of Egibi ; 35 shekels which have been mortgaged to Tabnea, the son of Nebo-yusallim, the son of Sin-sadunu, and 20 shekels which are due from Tasmetum-ramat, the daughter of Arad-Bel, the son of Egibi, as well as a field producing 48 qas of seed on the canal of Kish. As regards the maneh and 56 shekels belonging to Gugûa, which, in the absence of her eldest son, Ea-zir-ibni, she has divided between her younger sons, Nebo-akhi-bullidh, Nergal-ina-esi-edher, Itti-Samas-baladhu, and Ninip-pir-utsur, Ea-zir-ibni shall have no claim to them. Gugûa has delivered to Ea-zir-ibni, her eldest son, one maneh. now in the hands of Nebo-akhi-iddin, 55 shekels in the hands of Tabnea, 50 shekels in the hands of Tasmetum-ramat, and a field bearing 48 qas of seed. As long as Gugûa lives, Ea-zir-ibni shall give his mother Gugûa, as interest upon the property, food and clothing. Gugûa shall alienate none of it out of affection or will it away. Ea-zir-ibni shall not be disturbed in his possession." The names of three witnesses are attached to the deed, which was " sealed in the presence of Babâ, the daughter of Nebo-zir-lisir, the son of Egibi."

Another case in which a kind of will seems to have been made which should take effect during the lifetime of the testator, is a document drawn up by order of the Assyrian King Sennacherib. We may gather from it that Esar-haddon, though not his eldest, was his favorite son, a fact which may explain his subsequent assassination by two of his other sons, who took advantage of their brother's absence in Armenia at the head of the army, to murder their father and usurp the throne. In the document in question Sennacherib makes a written statement of his desire to leave to Esar-haddon certain personal effects, which are enumerated by name. "Gold rings, quantities of ivory, gold cups, dishes, and necklaces, all these valuable objects in plenty, as well as three sorts of precious stones, one and one-half maneh and two and one-half shekels in weight, I bequeath to Esar-haddon, my son, who bears the surname of Assur-etil-kin-pal, to be deposited in the house of Amuk." It will be noticed that this document is not attested by witnesses. Such attestation was dispensed with in the case of the monarch; his own name was sufficient to create a title. Whether it would have been the same in Babylonia, where the king was not equally autocratic and the commercial spirit was stronger than in Assyria, may be questioned. At all events, when Gigitu, the daughter of the Babylonian King Nergal-sharezer, was married to one of his officials, the contract was made out in the usual form, and the names of several witnesses were attached to it, while the deeds relating to the trading transactions of Belshazzar when heir-apparent to the throne differ in nothing from those required from the ordinary citizen.

Besides possessing the power of making a will, the head of the family was able to increase it by adoption. The practice of adoption was of long standing in Babylonia. The right to become King of Babylon and so to claim legitimate rule over the civilized world was conferred through adoption by the god Bel-Merodach. The claimant to sovereignty "took the hand of Bel," as it was termed, and thereby became the adopted son of the god. Until this ceremony was performed, however much he might be a sovereign *de facto*, he was not so *de jure*. The legal title to rule could be given by Bel, and by Bel alone. As the Pharaohs of Egypt were sons of Ra the Sun-god, so it was necessary that the kings of Babylon should be the sons of the Babylonian Sun-god Merodach. Sonship alone made them legitimate.

This theory of adoption by a god must have been derived from a practice that was already well known. And the power of adopting children was exercised by the Babylonians up to the last. It has been suggested that it was due to ancestor-worship, and the desire to prevent the customary offerings from being discontinued through the extinction of the family. But for this there is no evidence. Indeed, it is questionable whether there was any worship of ancestors in Babylonia except in the case of the royal family. And even here it had its origin in the deification of the kings during their lifetime.

The prevalence of adoption in Babylonia had a

much less recondite cause. It was one of the results
of the recognition of private property and the principle of individual ownership. The head of the
family naturally did not wish his estate to pass out
of it and be transferred to a stranger. Wherever
monogany is the general rule, the feeling of family
relationship is strong, and such was the case among
the Babylonians. The feeling shows itself in the
fact that when inherited land is sold we find other
members of the family signing their assent by their
presence at the sale. The father or mother, accordingly, who adopted a child did so with the intention
of making him their heir, and so keeping the estate
they had inherited or acquired in the hands of their
own kin.

That this is the true explanation of the Babylonian
practice of adoption is clear from the case mentioned
above in which Bel-Katsir was prevented from
adopting his step-son, because his uncle and adoptive
father, whose property would then have passed to the
latter, objected to his doing so. It was entirely a
question of inheritance. Bel-Katsir had been adopted
in order that he might be his uncle's heir, and consequently the uncle had the right of deciding to whom
his estate should ultimately go. He preferred that
it should be the brother of Bel-Katsir, and the brother
accordingly it was settled to be.

The fact that women could adopt, also points in the
same direction. The woman was the equal of the
man as regards the possession and management of
property, and like the man, therefore, she could determine who should inherit it.

A slave could be adopted as well as a free man. It was one of the ways in which a slave obtained his freedom, and contracts for the sale of slaves generally guarantee that they have not been adopted into the family of a citizen. A curious suit that was brought before a special court at Babylon in the tenth year of Nabonidos illustrates the advantage that was sometimes taken of the fact. The action was brought against a slave who bears the Israelitish name of Barachiel, and may, therefore, have been a Jew, and it was tried, not only before the ordinary judges, but before special commissioners and "elders" as well. The following is a translation of the judgment which was delivered and preserved in the record office :

"Barachiel is the slave of Gagâ, the daughter of . . . , redeemable with money only. In the thirty-fifth year of Nebuchadnezzar, King of Babylon (570 B.C.), he was given to Akhi-nuri, son of Nebo-nadin-akhi, as security for a debt of twenty-eight shekels. Now he claims that he is the adopted son of Bel-rimanni, who has joined the hands of Samas-mudam-miq, the son of Nebo-nadin-akhi, and Qudasu, the daughter of Akhi-nuri, in matrimony. The case was pleaded before the commissioners, the elders, and the judges of Nabonidos, King of Babylon, and the arguments were heard on both sides. They read the deeds relating to the servile condition of Barachiel, who from the thirty-fifth year of Nebuchadnezzar, King of Babylon, to the seventh year of Nabonidos, King of Babylon, had been sold for money, had been given as security for a debt, and had been handed over to Nubtâ, the daughter of Gagâ, as her dowry—Nubtâ

had afterward, by a sealed deed, given him with a
house and other slaves to her son, Zamama-iddin,
and her husband, Nadin-abla—and they said to
Barachiel: You have brought an action and called
yourself an adopted son. Prove to us your adoption.
Barachiel thereupon confessed: Twice did I run away
from the house of my master and for many days was
not seen. Then I was afraid and pretended to be an
adopted son. My adoption is non-existent; I was
the slave of Gagâ, redeemable with money. Nubtâ,
her daughter, made a present of me, and by a sealed
deed transferred me to her son, Zamama-iddin, and
her husband, Nadin-abla. After the death of Gagâ
and Nubtâ, I was sold by sealed contract to Itti-
Merodach-baladhu, the son of Nebo-akhi-iddin, the
son of Egibi. I will go and [perform each of my
duties. The commissioners,] the elders, and the
judges heard his evidence and restored him to his
servile condition, and [confirmed] his possession by
Samas-mudammiq [the son of Nebo-nadin-akhi] and
Qudasu, the daughter of Akhi-nuri, who had given
him as a dowry (to his daughter)." Then follow the
names of the judges and secretary, and the date and
place where the judgment was delivered, two of the
judges further affixing their seals to the document,
as well as a certain Kiribtu who calls himself "the
shield-bearer," but who was probably one of the
commissioners sent to investigate the case.

After a slave had been adopted, it was in the power
of the adoptive father to cancel the act of adoption
and reduce him to his former state of servitude if he
had not performed his part of the contract and the

parties who had witnessed it were willing that it
should be cancelled. We learn this from a deed that
was drawn up in the thirteenth year of Nabonidos.
Here we read:

"Iqisa-abla, the son of Kudurru, the son of Nur-Sin,
sealed a deed by which he adopted his servant.
Rimanni-Bel, usually called Rimut, in return for his
receiving food and clothing from Rimanni-Bel. But
Rimanni-Bel, usually called Rimut, has violated
the contract ever since the deed by which he was
adopted was sealed, and has given neither food, oil,
nor clothing, whereas Ê-Saggil-ramat, the daughter
of Ziria, the son of Nabâ, the wife of Nadin-Merodach,
the son of Iqisa-abla, the son of Nur-Sin, has taken
her father-in-law, has housed him, and has been kind
to him and has provided him with food, oil, and
clothing. Iqisa-abla, the son of Kudurru, the son of
Nur-Sin, has, therefore, of his own free will, cancelled
the deed of adoption, and by a sealed deed has given
Rimanni-Bel to wait upon Ê-Saggil-ramat and Nubtâ,
the daughter of Ê-Saggil-ramat and Nadin-Merodach,
the grandson of Nur-Sin; Ê Saggil-ramat and Nubtâ,
her daughter, shall he obey. After the death of Ê-
Saggil-ramat he shall wait on Nubtâ, her daughter.
Whoever shall change these words and shall destroy
the deed which Iqisa-abla has drawn up and given
to Ê-Saggil-ramat and Nubtâ, her daughter, may Merodach and the goddess Zarpanit denounce judgment
upon him!" Then come the names of four witnesses
and the clerk, the date and place of writing, and the
statement that the deed was indented in the presence
of Bissâ, the daughter of Iqisa-abla.

It is clear that the testator had little or no property of his own, and that he was too old, or otherwise incapacitated, to earn anything for himself. It is also clear that the adopted slave, who is described by the milder term *gallu*, or "servant," had acquired some wealth, and that this was the motive for his adoption. He, however, deserted and neglected his adopted father after his freedom had been secured to him, and thereby failed to carry out his part of the contract. Iqisa-abla accordingly had the legal right to break it also on his side.

One of the effects of the system of adoption was to give the privileges of Babylonian citizenship to a good many foreigners. The foreign origin of Barachiel, as evidenced by his name, was no obstacle to his claim to be a citizen, and the numerous contracts in which it is certified of a foreign slave that he has never been adopted prove the fact conclusively. A commercial community cannot afford to be exclusive on the ground of race and nationality.

Such, then, was the family system in the Babylonia of the historical period. Polygamy was rare, and the married woman possessed full rights over her property and could employ or bequeath it as she chose. The dowry she brought from her father or other near relation made her practically independent of her husband. Sons and daughters alike were able to inherit, and the possessor of property had the power of making a will. The law seems to have placed but few restrictions upon the way in which he could bestow his wealth. A family could be increased or prevented from dying out by means of adoption, and new blood could thus be introduced into it.

The rights and duties of the individual were fully recognized ; it was with him alone that the law had to deal.   Nevertheless, a few traces survived of that doctrine of the solidarity of the family which had preceded the development of individual ownership and freedom of action.   The bride was given in marriage by her parents, or, failing these, by her nearest male relations, and when an estate was sold which had long been in the possession of a certain family, it was customary for the rest of the family to signify their consent by attending the sale.   We may gather, however, that the sale was not invalidated if the consent was not obtained.   In the older days of Babylonian history, moreover, it was usual for the property of a deceased citizen to be divided among his heirs without the intervention of a will.   It went in the first instance to his widow, and was then divided equally among his children, whether body heirs or adopted ones, the eldest son alone receiving an additional share in return for administering the estate. But disputes frequently arose over the division, and the members of the family went to law with one another.   In such cases it became the custom to place the whole of the property in the hands of the priests of the city-temple, who thus corresponded to the English Court of Chancery, and made the division as they judged best.   The results, however, were not always satisfactory, and it was doubtless in order to avoid both the litigation and the necessity of appointing executors who were not members of the

family, that the will came to play so important a part
in the succession to property. In bequeathing his
possessions the head of the family was expected to
observe the usual rule of division, but it ceased to
be obligatory to do so.

CHAPTER III

EDUCATION AND DEATH

ONE of the lesson-books used in the Babylonian nursery contains the beginning of a story, written in Sumerian and translated into Semitic, which describes the adventures of a foundling who was picked up in the streets and adopted by the King. We are told that he was taken "from the mouth of the dogs and ravens," and was then brought to the *asip* or "prophet," who marked the soles of his feet with his seal. What the precise object of this procedure was it is difficult to say, but the custom is alluded to in the Old Testament (Job xiii. 27). Certain tribes in the south of China still brand the soles of a boy's feet, for the purpose, it is said, of testing his strength and hardihood.

After the operation was performed the boy was handed over to a "nurse," to whom his "bread, food, shirt, and (other) clothing were assured for three years." At the same time, we may assume, he received a name. This giving of a name was an important event in the child's life. Like other nations of antiquity the Babylonians conformed the name with the person who bore it; it not only represented him, but in a sense was actually himself. Magical

44

properties were ascribed to the name, and it thus became of importance to know what names were good or bad, lucky or unlucky. An unlucky name brought evil fortune to its possessor, a lucky name secured his success in life. A change of name influenced a man's career; and the same superstitious belief which caused the Cape of Storms to become the Cape of Good Hope not unfrequently occasioned a person's name to be altered among the nations of the ancient East.

The gods themselves were affected by the names they bore. A knowledge of the secret and ineffable name of a deity was the key to a knowledge of his inner essence and attributes, and conferred a power over him upon the fortunate possessor of it. The patron god of the dynasty to which Khammurabi belonged was spoken of as "the Name," Sumu or Samu, the Shem of the Old Testament; his real title was too sacred to be uttered in speech. The name of a thing was the thing itself, and so too the name of a god or person was the actual god or person to whom it was attached.

A large proportion of Babylonian names includes the name of some divinity. In spite of their length and unwieldiness they tended to increase in number as time went on. In ordinary life, however, they were frequently shortened. In the contract given in the last chapter, the slave Rimanni-Bel is said to have been usually called Rimut, the one name signifying "Love me, O Bel," the other "Love." In other instances we find Samas-musezib contracted into Samsiya and Suzub, Kabti-ilâni-Merodach into

Kabtiya, Nebo-tabni-uzur into Tabniya. The Bele-
sys of Greek writers is the Babylonian Balasu,
which is a shortened form of Merodach-balasu-iqbi,
and Baladan, which is given in the Old Testament as
the name of the father of Merodach-baladan, has lost
the name of the god with which it must originally
have begun.

Sometimes a change in the form of the name was
due to its being of foreign origin and consequently
mispronounced by the Babylonians, who assimilated
it to words in their own language. Thus Sargon of
Akkad was properly called Sargani, "The Strong One,"
or, more fully, Sargani-sar-ali, "Sargani, the King of
the City," but his Sumerian subjects turned this into
Sar-gina or Sargon, "The Established King." The
grandson of Khammurabi bore the Canaanitish name
of Abesukh, the Abishua of the Israelites, "The
Father of Welfare," but it was transformed by the
Babylonians into Ebisum, which in their own dialect
meant "The Actor." Eri-Aku or Arioch was an
Elamite name signifying "The Servant of the Moon-
god;" the Babylonians changed it into Rim-Sin and
perhaps even Rim-Anu, "Love, O Moon-god,"
"Love, O Sky-god."

At other times the name was changed for political
or superstitious reasons. When the successful general
Pul usurped the throne of Assyria he adopted the
name of one of the most famous of the kings of the
older dynasty, Tiglath-pileser. His successor, another
usurper, called Ululâ, similarly adopted the name of
Shalmaneser, another famous king of the earlier
dynasty. It is probable that Sargon, who was also

a usurper, derived ·his name from Sargon of Akkad, and that his own name was originally something else. Sennacherib tells us that Esar-haddon had a second name, or surname, by which he was known to his neighbors. In this respect he was like Solomon of Israel, who was also called Jedidiah.

It is doubtful whether circumcision was practised in Babylonia. There is no reference to it in the inscriptions, nor is it mentioned by classical writers as among Babylonian customs. In fact, the words of the Greek historian Herodotus seem to exclude the practice, as the Babylonians are not one of the nations of Western Asia who are said by him to have learnt the rite from the Egyptians. Moreover, Abraham and his family were not circumcised until long after he had left Babylonia and had established himself in Canaan. Africa, rather than Asia, seems to have been the original home of the rite.

If the boy were the son of well-to-do parents he was sent to school at an early age. One of the texts which, in Sumerian days, was written as a head-line in his copy-book declared that "He who would excel in the school of the scribes must rise like the dawn." Girls also shared in the education given to their brothers. Among the Babylonian letters that have been preserved are some from ladies, and the very fact that women could transact business on their own account implies that they could read and write. Thus the following letter, written from Babylon by a lover to his mistress at Sippara, assumes that she could read it and return an answer: "To the lady Kasbeya thus says Gimil-Merodach: May the Sun-god and Merodach, for my sake, grant thee everlasting life! I am writing to enquire after your health; please send me news of it. I am living at Babylon, but have not seen you, which troubles me greatly. Send me news of your arrival, so that I may be happy. Come in the month Marchesvan. May you live forever, for my sake!" The Tel-el-Amarna collection actually contains letters from a lady to the Egyptian Pharaoh. One of them is as follows: "To the king my lord, my gods, my sun-god, thus says Nin, thy handmaid: At the feet of the king my lord, my gods, my sun-god, seven times seven I prostrate myself. The king my lord knows that there is war in the land, and that all the country of the king my lord has revolted to the Bedâwin. But the king my lord has knowledge of his country, and the king my lord knows that the Bedâwin have sent to the city of Ajalon and to the city of Zorah, and have made mischief (and have intrigued with) the two sons of Malchiel; and let the king my lord take knowledge of this fact."

The oracles delivered to Esar-haddon by the prophetesses of Arbela are in writing, and we have no grounds for thinking that they were written down by an uninspired pen. Indeed, the "bit riduti," or "place of education," where Assur-bani-pal tells us he had been brought up, was the woman's part of the palace. The instructors, however, were men, and part of the boy's education, we are informed, consisted in his being taught to shoot with the bow and to practise other bodily exercises. But the larger part of his time was given to learning how to read and write.

The acquisition of the cuneiform system of writing was a task of labor and difficulty which demanded years of patient application. A vast number of characters had to be learned by heart. They were conventional signs, often differing but slightly from one another, with nothing about them that could assist the memory; moreover, their forms varied in different styles of writing, as much as Latin, Gothic, and cursive forms of type differ among ourselves, and all these the pupil was expected to know. Every character had more than one phonetic value; many of them, indeed, had several, while they could also be used ideographically to express objects and ideas. But this was not all. A knowledge of the cuneiform syllabary necessitated also a knowledge of the language of the Sumerians, who had been its inventors, and it frequently happened that a group of characters which had expressed a Sumerian word was retained in the later script with the pronunciation of the corresponding Semitic word attached to them, though the latter had nothing to do with the phonetic values of the several signs, whether pronounced singly or as a whole.

The children, however, must have been well taught. This is clear from the remarkably good spelling which we find in the private letters; it is seldom that words are misspelt. The language may be conversational, or even dialectic, but the words are written correctly. The school-books that have survived bear testimony to the attention that had been given to improving the educational system. Every means was adopted for lessening the labor of the student and imprinting the lesson upon his mind. The cuneiform characters had been classified and named; they had also been arranged according to the number and position of the separate wedges of which they consisted. Dictionaries had been compiled of Sumerian words and expressions, as well as lists of Semitic synonyms. Even grammars had been drawn up, in which the grammatical forms of the old language of Sumer were interpreted in Semitic Babylonian. There were reading-books filled with extracts from the standard literature of the country. Most of this was in Sumerian; but the Sumerian text was provided with a Semitic translation, sometimes interlinear, sometimes in a parallel column. Commentaries, moreover, had been written upon the works of ancient authors, in which difficult or obsolete terms were explained. The pupils were trained to write exercises, either from a copy placed before them or from memory. These exercises served a double purpose—they taught the pupil how to write and spell, as well as the subject which the exercise illustrated. A list of the kings of the dynasty to which Khammurabi belonged has come to us, for instance, in one of them. In this way history and geography were impressed upon the student's memory, together with extracts from the poets and prose-writers of the past.

The writing material was clay. Papyrus, it is true, was occasionally used, but it was expensive, while clay literally lay under the feet of everyone. While the clay was still soft, the cuneiform or "wedge-shaped" characters were engraved upon it by means

of a stylus. They had originally been pictorial, but
when the use of clay was adopted the pictures necessarily degenerated into groups of wedge-like lines,
every curve becoming an angle formed by the junc-
tion of two lines. As time went on, the characters
were more and more simplified, the number of
wedges of which they consisted being reduced and
only so many left as served to distinguish one sign
from another. The simplification reached its ex-
treme point in the official script of Assyria.

At first the clay tablet after being inscribed was
allowed to dry in the sun. But sun-dried clay easily
crumbles, and the fashion accordingly grew up of
baking the tablet in a kiln. In Assyria, where the
heat of the sun was not so great as in the southern kingdom of Babylonia, the tablet was invariably
baked, holes being first drilled in it to allow the
escape of the moisture and to prevent it from crack-
ing. Some of the early Babylonian tablets were of
great size, and it is wonderful that they have lasted
to our own days. But the larger the tablet, the more
difficult it was to bake it safely, and consequently
the most of the tablets are of small size. As it was
often necessary to compress a long text into this lim-
ited space, the writing became more and more minute,
and in many cases a magnifying glass is needed to
read it properly. That such glasses were really used
by the Assyrians is proved by Layard's discovery of
a magnifying lens at Nineveh. The lens, which is of
crystal, has been turned on a lathe, and is now in the
British Museum. But even with the help of lenses,
the study of the cuneiform tablets encouraged short

sight, which must have been common in the Babylonian schools.   In the case of Assur-bani-pal this
was counteracted by the out-of-door exercises in
which he was trained, and it is probable that similar
exercises were also customary in Babylonia.

A book generally consisted of several tablets, which
may consequently be compared with our chapters.
At the end of each tablet was a colophon stating what
was its number in the series to which it belonged,
and giving the first line of the next tablet.   The
series received its name from the words with which
it began; thus the fourth tablet or chapter of the
"Epic of the Creation " states that it contains " one
hundred and forty-six lines of the fourth tablet (of
the work beginning) ' When on high unproclaimed,' "
and adds the first line of the tablet which follows.
Catalogues were made of the standard books to be
found in a library, giving the name of the author
and the first line of each; so that it was easy for the
reader or librarian to find both the work he wanted
and the particular chapter in it he wished to consult.
The books were arranged on shelves ; M. de Sarzec
discovered about 32,000 of them at Tello in Southern
Chaldea still in the order in which they had been put
in the age of Gudea (2700 B.C.).

Literature of every kind was represented.   History and chronology, geography and law, private and
public correspondence, despatches from generals and
proclamations of the king, philology and mathematics,
natural science in the shape of lists of bears and birds,
insects and stones, astronomy and astrology, theology
and the pseudo-science of omens, all found a place

on the shelves, as well as poems and purely literary works.   Copies of deeds and contracts, of legal decisions, and even inventories of the property of private individuals, were also stored in the libraries of Babylonia and Assyria, which were thus libraries and archive-chambers in one.   In Babylonia every great city had its collection of books, and scribes were kept constantly employed in it, copying and re-editing the older literature, or providing new works for readers. The re-editing was done with scrupulous care. Where a character was lost in the original text by a fracture of the tablet, the copyist stated the fact, and added whether the loss was recent or not.   Where the form of the character was uncertain, both the signs which it resembled are given.   Some idea may be formed of the honesty and care with which the Babylonian scribes worked from the fact that the compiler of the Babylonian Chronicle, which contains a synopsis of later Babylonian history, frankly states that he does " not know " the date of the battle of Khalulê, which was fought between the Babylonians and Sennacherib.   The materials at his disposal did not enable him to settle it.   It so happens that we are in a more fortunate position, as we are able to fix it with the help of the annals of the Assyrian King.

New texts were eagerly collected.   The most precious spoils sent to Assur-bani-pal after the capture of the revolted Babylonian cities were tablets containing works which the library of Nineveh did not possess.   The Babylonians and Assyrians made war upon men, not upon books, which were, moreover, under the protection of the gods. The library was usually within the walls of a temple; sometimes it was part of the archives of the temple itself. Hence the copying of a text was often undertaken as a pious work, which brought down upon the scribe the blessing of heaven and even the remission of his sins. That the library was open to the public we may infer from the character of some of the literature contained in it. This included private letters as well as contracts and legal documents which could be interesting only to the parties whom they concerned.

The school must have been attached to the library, and was probably an adjacent building. This will explain the existence of the school-exercises which have come from the library of Nineveh, as well as the reading-books and other scholastic literature which were stored within it. At the same time, when we remember the din of an oriental school, where the pupils shout their lessons at the top of their voices, it is impossible to suppose that the scribes and readers would have been within ear-shot. Nor was it probable that there was only one school in a town of any size. The practice of herding large numbers of boys or girls together in a single school-house is European rather than Asiatic.

The school in later times developed into a university. At Borsippa, the suburb of Babylon, where the library had been established in the temple of Nebo, we learn from Strabo that a university also existed which had attained great celebrity. From a fragment of a Babylonian medical work, now in the British

Museum, we may perhaps infer that it was chiefly celebrated as a school of medicine.

In Assyria education was mainly confined to the upper classes. The trading classes were perforce obliged to learn how to read and write; so also were the officials and all those who looked forward to a career in the diplomatic service. But learning was regarded as peculiarly the profession of the scribes, who constituted a special class and occupied an important position in the bureaucracy. They acted as clerks and secretaries in the various departments of state, and stereotyped a particular form of cuneiform script, which we may call the chancellor's hand, and which, through their influence, was used throughout the country. In Babylonia it was otherwise. Here a knowledge of writing was far more widely spread, and one of the results was that varieties of handwriting became as numerous as they are in the modern world. The absence of a professional class of scribes prevented any one official hand from becoming universal. We find even the son of an "irrigator," one of the poorest and lowest members of the community, copying a portion of the "Epic of the Creation," and depositing it in the library of Borsippa for the good of his soul. Indeed, the contract tablets show that the slaves themselves could often read and write. The literary tendencies of Assur-bani-pal doubtless did much toward the spread of education in Assyria, but the latter years of his life were troubled by disastrous wars, and the Assyrian empire and kingdom came to an end soon after his death.

Education, as we have seen, meant a good deal more

than merely learning the cuneiform characters. It
meant, in the case of the Semitic Babylonians and
Assyrians, learning the ancient agglutinative language
of Sumer as well. In later times this language ceased
to be spoken except in learned society, and consequently bore the same relation to Semitic Babylonian
that Latin bears to English. In learning Sumerian,
therefore, the Babylonian learned what was equivalent
to Latin in the modern world. And the mode of
teaching it was much the same. There were the same
paradigms to be committed to memory, the same lists
of words and phrases to be learned by heart, the same
extracts from the authors of the past to be stored up
in the mind. Even the "Hamiltonian" system of
learning a dead language had already been invented.
Exercises were set in translation from Sumerian
into Babylonian, and from Babylonian into Sumerian,
and the specimens of the latter which have survived
to us show that "dog-Latin" was not unknown.

But the dead language of Sumer was not all that
the educated Babylonian or Assyrian gentlemen of
later times was called upon to know. In the eighth
century before our era Aramaic had become the common medium of trade and diplomacy. If Sumerian
was the Latin of the Babylonian world, Aramaic was
its French. The Aramaic dialects seem to have been
the result of a contact between the Semitic languages
of Arabia and Canaan, and the rising importance of
the tribes who spoke them and who occupied Mesopotamia and Northern Arabia caused them to become
the language of trade. Aramaic merchants were
settled on the banks of the Euphrates and Tigris,

and conveyed the products of Babylonia and Phœnicia from one country to the other. Many of the commercial firms in Babylonia were of Aramaic origin,
and it was natural that some part at least of their business should have been carried on in the language of
their fathers.

Hence it was that, when the Rab-shakeh or Vizier
of Sennacherib appeared before Jerusalem and summoned its inhabitants to submit to the Assyrian King,
he was asked by the ministers of Hezekiah to speak
in "Aramæan."   It was taken for granted that
Aramaic was known to an Assyrian official and diplo-
matist just as it was to the Jewish officials themselves. The Rab-shakeh, however, knew the Hebrew
language as well, and found it more to his purpose to
use it in addressing the Jews.

Here, then, we have an Assyrian officer who is acquainted not only with Sumerian, but also with two
of the living languages of Western Asia. And yet
he was not a scribe ; he did not belong to the professional class of learned men. Nothing can show more
clearly the advanced state of education even in the
military kingdom of Assyria. In Babylonia learning
had always been honored ; from the days of Sargon
of Akkad onward the sons of the reigning king did
not disdain to be secretaries and librarians.

The linguistic training undergone in the schools
gave the Babylonian a taste for philology. He not
only compiled vocabularies of the extinct Sumerian,
which were needed for practical reasons, he also
explained the meaning of the names of the foreign
kings who had reigned over Babylonia, and from

time to time noted the signification of words belonging to the various languages by which he was surrounded. Thus one of the tablets we possess contains a list of Kassite or Kossean words with their
signification; in other cases we have Mitannian,
Elamite, and Canaanite words quoted, with their
meanings attached to them. Nor did the philological
curiosity of the scribe end here. He busied himself
with the etymology of the words in his own language,
and just as a couple of centuries ago our own dic-
tionary-makers endeavored to find derivations for all
English words, whatever their source, in Latin and
Greek, so, too, the Babylonian etymologist believed
that the venerable language of Sumer was the key to
the origin of his own. Many of the words in Semitic
Babylonian were indeed derived from it, and accordingly Sumerian etymologies were found for other
words which were purely Semitic. The word *Sabattu*,
"the Sabbath," for instance, was derived from the
Sumerian *Sa*, "heart," and *bat*, "to cease," and so
interpreted to mean the day on which "the heart
ceased" from its labors.

History, too, was a favorite subject of study. Like
the Hebrews, the Assyrians were distinguished by a
keen historical sense which stands in curious contrast
to the want of it which characterized the Egyptian.
The Babylonians also were distinguished by the same
quality, though perhaps to a less extent than their
Assyrian neighbors, whose somewhat pedantic ac-
curacy led them to state the exact numbers of the
slain and captive in every small skirmish, and the
name of every petty prince with whom they came

into contact, and who had invented a system of accurately registering dates at a very early period. Nevertheless, the Babylonian was also a historian; the necessities of trade had obliged him to date his deeds and contracts from the earliest age of his history, and to compile lists of kings and dynasties for reference in case of a disputed title to property. The historical honesty to which he had been trained is illustrated by the author of the Babylonian Chronicle in the passage relating to the battle of Khalulê, which has been already alluded to. The last king of Babylonia was himself an antiquarian, and had a passion for excavating and discovering the records of the monarchs who had built the great temples of Chaldea.

Law, again, must have been much studied, and so, too, was theology. The library of Nineveh, however, from which so much of our information has come, gives us an exaggerated idea of the extent to which the pseudo-science of omens and portents was cultivated. Its royal patron was a believer in them, and apparently more interested in the subject than in any other. Consequently, the number of books relating to it are out of all proportion to the rest of the literature in the library. But this was an accident, due to the predilections of Assur-bani-pal himself.

The study of omens and portents was a branch of science and not of theology, false though the science was. But it was based upon the scientific principle that every antecedent has a consequent, its fallacy consisting in a confusion between real causes and mere antecedents. Certain events had been observed

to follow certain phenomena; it was accordingly
assumed that they were the results of the phenomena, and that were the phenomena to happen again
they would be followed by the same results. Hence
all extraordinary or unusual occurrences were carefully noted, together with whatever had been observed to come after them. A strange dog, for
instance, had been observed to enter a palace and
there lie down on a couch; as no disaster took place
subsequently it was believed that if the occurrence
was repeated it would be an omen of good fortune.
On the other hand, the fall of a house had been preceded by the birth of a child without a mouth; the
same result, it was supposed, would again accompany
the same presage of evil. These pseudo-scientific
observations had been commenced at a very early
period of Babylonian history, and were embodied in
a great work which was compiled for the library of
Sargon of Akkad.

Another work compiled for the same library, and
containing observations which started from a similarly
fallacious theory, was one in seventy-two books on the
pseudo-science of astrology, which was called "The
Illumination of Bel." But in this case the observations were not wholly useless. The study of astrology
was intermixed with that of astronomy, of which
Babylonia may be considered to be the birthplace.
The heavens had been mapped out and the stars
named; the sun's course along the ecliptic had
been divided into the twelve zodiacal signs, and
a fairly accurate calendar had been constructed.
Hundreds of observations had been made of the

eclipses of the sun and moon, and the laws reg-
ulating them had been so far ascertained that, first,
eclipses of the moon, and then, but with a greater
element of uncertainty, eclipses of the sun, were
able to be predicted. One of the chapters or books
in the "Illumination of Bel" was devoted to an
account of comets, another dealt with conjunctions
of the sun and moon. There were also tables of
observations relating to the synodic revolution of the
moon and the synodic periods of the planet Venus.
The year was divided into twelve months of thirty
days each, an intercalary month being inserted from
time to time to rectify the resulting error in the
length of the year. The months had been originally
called after the signs of the zodiac, whose names
have come down to ourselves with comparatively little change. But by the side of the lunar year
the Babylonians also used a sidereal year, the star
Capella being taken as a fixed point in the sky, from
which the distance of the sun could be measured at
the beginning of the year, the moon being used as a
mere pointer for the purpose. At a later date, however, this mode of determining time was abandoned,
and the new year was made directly dependent on
the vernal equinox. The month was subdivided into
weeks of seven days, each of which was consecrated
to a particular deity.

These deities were further identified with the stars.
The fact that the sun and moon, as well as the evening and morning stars, were already worshipped as
divinities doubtless led the way to this system of
astro-theology. But it seems never to have spread

beyond the learned classes and to have remained to
the last an artificial system. The mass of the people
worshipped the stars as a whole, but it was only as
a whole and not individually. Their identification
with the gods of the state religion might be taught
in the schools and universities, but it had no meaning for the nation at large.

From the beginning of the Babylonian's life we
now pass to the end. Unlike the Egyptian he had
no desert close at hand in which to bury his dead,
no limestone cliffs, as in Palestine, wherein a tomb
might be excavated. It was necessary that the
burial should be in the plain of Babylonia, the same
plain as that in which he lived, and with which
the overflow of the rivers was constantly infiltrating.
The consequences were twofold. On the one hand,
the tomb had to be constructed of brick, for stone
was not procurable; on the other hand, sanitary reasons made cremation imperative. The Babylonian
corpse was burned as well as buried, and the brick
sepulchre that was raised above it adjoined the cities
of the living.

The corpse was carried to the grave on a bier, accompanied by the mourners. Among these the wail-
ing women were prominent, who tore their hair and
threw dust upon their heads. The cemetery to
which the dead was carried was a city in itself, to
which the Sumerians had given the name of Ki-makh
or "vast place." It was laid out in streets, the tombs
on either side answering to the houses of a town.
Not infrequently gardens were planted before them,
while rivulets of "living water" flowed through the

streets and were at times conducted into the tomb. The water symbolized the life that the pious Babylonian hoped to enjoy in the world to come. It relieved the thirst of the spirit in the underground world of Hades, where an old myth had declared that "dust only was its food," and it was at the same time an emblem of those " waters of life " which were believed to bubble up beneath the throne of the goddess of the dead.

When the corpse reached the cemetery it was laid upon the ground wrapped in mats of reed and covered with asphalt. It was still dressed in the clothes and ornaments that had been worn during life. The man had his seal and his weapons of bronze or stone; the woman her spindle-wheel and thread; the child his necklace of shells. In earlier times all was then thickly coated with clay, above which branches of palm, terebinth, and other trees were placed, and the whole was set on fire. At a more recent period ovens of brick were constructed in which the corpse was put in its coffin of clay and reeds, but withdrawn before cremation was complete. The skeletons of the dead are consequently often found in a fair state of preservation, as well as the objects which were buried with them.

While the body was being burned offerings were made, partly to the gods, partly to the dead man himself. They consisted of dates, calves and sheep, birds and fish, which were consumed along with the corpse. Certain words were recited at the same time, derived for the most part from the sacred books of ancient Sumer.

After the ceremony was over a portion of the ashes was collected and deposited in an urn, if the cremation had been complete. In the later days, when this was not the case, the half-burnt body was allowed to remain on the spot where it had been laid, and an aperture was made in the shell of clay with which it was covered. The aperture was intended to allow a free passage to the spirit of the dead, so that it might leave its burial-place to enjoy the food and water that were brought to it. Over the whole a tomb was built of bricks, similar to that in which the urn was deposited when the body was completely burned.

The tombs of the rich resembled the houses in which they had lived on earth and contained many chambers. In these their bodies were cremated and interred. Sometimes a house was occupied by a single corpse only; at other times it became a family burial-place, where the bodies were laid in separate chambers. Sometimes tombstones were set up commemorating the name and deeds of the deceased; at other times statues representing them were erected instead.

The tomb had a door, like a house, through which the relatives and friends of the dead man passed from time to time in order to furnish him with the food and sustenance needed by his spirit in the world below. Vases were placed in the sepulchre, filled with dates and grain, wine and oil, while the rivulet which flowed beside it provided water in abundance. All this was required in that underworld where popular belief pictured the dead as flitting like bats in the gloom and darkness, and where the heroes of old time sat, strengthless and ghostlike, on their shadowy thrones.

The kings were allowed to be burned and buried in the palace in which they had lived and ruled. We read of one of them that he was interred in " the palace of Sargon " of Akkad, of another that his burial had taken place in the palace he himself had erected. A similar privilege was granted to their subjects only by royal permission.

Want of space caused the tombs of the dead to be built one upon the other, as generations passed away and the older sepulchres crumbled into dust. The cemetery thus resembled the city ; here, too, one generation built upon the ruins of its predecessor. The houses and tombs were alike constructed of sundried bricks, which soon disintegrate and form a mound of dust. The age of a cemetery, like the age of a city, may accordingly be measured by the number of successive layers of building of which its mound or platform is composed. In Babylonia they are numerous, for the history of the country goes back to a remote past. Each city clustered round a temple, venerable for its antiquity as well as for its sanctity, and the cemetery which stood near it was consequently under the protection of its god. At Cutha the necropolis was so vast that Nergal, the god of the town, came to be known as the "lord of the dead." But the cemeteries of other towns were also of enormous size. Western Asia had received its culture and the elements of its theology from Babylonia, and Babylonia consequently was a sacred land not only to the Babylonians themselves, but to

all those who shared their civilization. The very
soil was holy ground; Assyrians as well as Babylonians desired that their bodies should rest in it.
Here they were in the charge, as it were, of Bel of
Nippur or Merodach of Babylon, and within sight
of the ancient sanctuaries in which those gods were
worshipped. This explains in part the size of the
cemeteries; the length of time during which they
were used will explain the rest. As Dr. Peters says
of each:[1] "It is difficult to convey anything like a
correct notion of the piles upon piles of human relics
which there utterly astound the spectator. Excepting only the triangular space between the three principal ruins, the whole remainder of the platform, the
whole space between the walls, and an unknown
extent of desert beyond them, are everywhere filled
with the bones and sepulchres of the dead. There is
probably no other site in the world which can compare with Warka in this respect."

Babylonia is still a holy land to the people of
Western Asia. The old feeling in regard to it still
survives, and the bodies of the dead are still carried,
sometimes for hundreds of miles, to be buried in its
sacred soil. Mohammedan saints have taken the
place of the old gods, and a Moslem chapel represents
the temple of the past, but it is still to Babylonia
that the corpse is borne, often covered by costly rugs
which find their way in time to an American or
European drawing-room. "The old order changes,
giving place to new," but the influence of Chaldean
culture and religion is not yet past.

[1] Journal of the American Oriental Society, xviii., p. 167.

CHAPTER IV

SLAVERY was part of the foundation upon which Babylonian society rested. But between slavery as it existed in the ancient oriental world and slavery in the Roman or modern world there was a great difference. The slave was often of the same race as his master, sometimes of the same nationality, speaking the same language and professing the same religion. He was regarded as one of the family, and was not infrequently adopted into it. He could become a free citizen and rise to the highest offices of state. Slavery was no bar to his promotion, nor did it imprint any stigma upon him. He was frequently a skilled artisan and even possessed literary knowledge. Between his habits and level of culture and those of his owners was no marked distinction, no prejudices to be overcome on account of his color, no conviction of his inferiority in race. He was brought up with the rest of the family to which he was considered to belong and was in hourly contact with them. Moreover, the large number of slaves had been captives in war. A reverse of fortune might consign their present masters to the same lot; history knew of instances in which master and slave had changed places

67

with one another. There were some slaves, too, who were Babylonians by birth; the law allowed the parent to sell his child, the brother his sister, or the creditor his debtor under certain circumstances, and the old Sumerian legislation ordained that a son who denied his father should be shorn and sold as a slave. In times of famine or necessity a man even sold himself to be quit of a debt or to obtain the means of subsistence. A slave was always fed and clothed; the free laborer at times could get neither food nor clothing.

There were three classes of slaves—those who were the property of a private individual, the serfs who were attached to the soil which they cultivated, and the temple slaves who had been dedicated to the service of the gods. Of the second class but few traces are found in Babylonia. Agriculture was carried on there either by free laborers, or by the slaves of the private land-owners. Where the land belonged to priests, it was of course usually the temple slaves who tilled it. What was the exact legal position of the Jews and other exiles who were transported to Babylonia by Nebuchadnezzar we do not know, but they were neither serfs nor slaves. The practice of transportation had been borrowed from Assyria, and under the Assyrian system the exiled population was treated as a colony. Israelites appear among the Assyrian officials in contracts of the second Assyrian empire, and Jewish names are found in the Babylonian contracts of the age of Nebuchadnezzar and his successors.

The Babylonians were not a military people, and

after the Kassite conquest their wars of aggression
were not sufficiently numerous or extensive to provide them with a supply of captives who could be
made into slaves. Slave-merchants are rarely, if
ever, referred to in the Babylonian contract tablets,
and the slaves must have been home-born, the children and descendants of those who had been slaves
before them. In the age of Abraham it was doubtless different. Then the power of Babylonia extended
throughout Western Asia, and the constant wars in
the East and West must have filled the market with
foreign captives. The white slaves brought from
Kurdistan and the north were especially prized.
Thus in the reign of Ammi-Zadok, the fourth successor of Khammurabi, some " white Kurdish
slaves " were sold for 3 homers and 24⅔ *qas* of oil,
which were valued at 20⅔ shekels, and in the time
of his son Samsu-ditana " a white slave " from Suri
or Northern Mesopotamia fetched as much as 20
shekels, or £3.

The earliest code of Sumerian laws known to us
takes the slave under its protection. It assumes the
principle that the life of the slave is not absolutely
at his master's disposal, and enacts that, if the slave
is killed, beaten, maimed, or injured in health, the
hand that has so offended shall pay each day a measure of wheat. This must mean that the payment
shall be continued until the slave recovers from his
ill-treatment. Light is thrown upon it by a later
Babylonian law, according to which, if the services of
a slave have been hired by a second person and the
slave falls ill or is otherwise rendered incapable of

work, the hirer is fined for as long a time as the ill-
ness or incapacity continues. The object of the law
is clear. It was intended to prevent the slave from
being overworked by one who had not, as it were, a
family interest in him. It protected the slave and at
the same time protected the master to whom he belonged.

There are several instances of its application.
Thus in the eighth year of Cyrus a slave named Nidinti was apprenticed for six years by his master and
mistress to a certain Libludh in order that he might
learn the trade of fulling. It was stipulated that
he was to learn it thoroughly, and if at any time he
was unable to work Libludh was to pay each day
3 *qas* (or about 4½ quarts) of wheat for his support.
At the end of the period, when the trade had been
learned, Libludh was to receive a cloth worth 4
shekels (12 s.) and hand over Nidinti to the service of
the Sun-god of Sippara. In the same year another
slave was apprenticed to the stone-cutter Quddâ, who
was himself a slave and belonged to the heir-apparent, Cambyses. Quddâ undertook to teach his trade
to the apprentice in four years, and if he failed to do
so was to be fined 20 shekels. Six years earlier
Qubtâ, the daughter of Iddina-Merodach, had given
the slave of another person to a weaver for a period
of five years, in order that he might be taught the art
of weaving, at the same time agreeing to provide
him with 1 *qa* (1¾ quarts) of food each day and to
pay his teacher something besides. If, however, he
was incapacitated from learning, the weaver was required to pay a daily fine of half a " measure " of

wheat, which we are told was the wage of the slave.
Any infringement of the contract would be punished
by a penalty of 20 manehs.

The slave was able to apprentice himself without
the intervention of his owners. Thus in the sixth
year of Cyrus one slave apprenticed himself of his
own accord to another in order to learn a trade. In
this case also the penalty for not being taught the
trade was half a "measure" of wheat each day, which
is again stated to be the wage of the slave. The
wage, however, it would seem, had to be paid to the
master, at all events in some cases; this is clear
from a document which relates to the conclusion of
the apprenticeship in which Nubtâ took part. The
slave she had apprenticed had learnt his trade, and
his master accordingly received from the teacher 5
shekels, which it was calculated were the equivalent
of the services the apprentice had rendered. Ordi-
narily the 5 shekels would have been considered a
return for the slave's maintenance during the term
of his apprenticeship; but in this instance, for reasons unknown to us, the maintenance had been provided by a lady and the payment for the slave's
services was consequently clear gain.

The slave, however, was allowed to accumulate
capital for himself, to trade with it, and even to become rich enough to lend money to his own master
or to purchase his own freedom. That a similar
privilege was allowed to the slaves of the Israelites
we may gather from the fact that Saul's slave offered to pay the seer Samuel a quarter of a shekel
which he had about him, though it is true that this

might have been the property of his master. In
Babylonia the possession of property by the slave
was not at all uncommon. In the sixth year of
Cambyses, for example, a female slave named
Khunnatu received a large quantity of furniture,
including five beds, ten chairs, three dishes, and
various other kitchen utensils, and agreed to pay
the rent of the house in which she deposited them.
Her master also lent her 122 shekels of silver,
which were expended in buying fifty casks of beer,
besides other things, and upon which she was to
pay interest. Apparently she wanted to set up
an inn or drinking-shop ; the fact that the money
was lent to her by her master proves that she
must have been engaged in business on her own
account. In other contracts we find the slave taking a mortgage and trading in onions and grain or
employing his money in usury. In one case a slave
borrows as much as 14 manehs 49 shekels, or
£138 3s., from a member of the Egibi firm. In another case it is a considerable quantity of grain in
addition to 12 shekels of silver that is borrowed
from the slave by two other persons, with a promise
that the grain shall be repaid the following month
and the money a year later. The contract is drawn
up in the usual way, the borrowers, who, like the
witnesses, are free-born citizens, giving the creditor
a security and assuming a common responsibility for
the debt. The grain, however, was to be repaid in
the house of the slave's master ; it seems evident,
therefore, that the slave had no private house of his
own. The slave, nevertheless, could own a house or

receive it in payment of a debt.   This is illustrated
by an interesting contract in which reference is made
to Ustanni, the Tatnai of the Book of Ezra, who is
called "the governor of Ebir-nâri," "the other side
of the river."   The contract is as follows :
"Two manehs of silver lent by Kurrulâ, the slave
of Ustanni, the governor of Babylon and Ebir-nâri, to
Merodach-sum-ibni, the son of Sula, the son of Epes-
ilu.   The house of the latter, which is by the side of
the road of the god Bagarus, is Kurrulâ's security.
No one else has any prior claim to it.   The house is
not to be let or interest taken upon the loan."   Then
come the names of five free-born witnesses, and the
document is dated at Babylon in the third year of
Darius.   The terms of the contract are precisely the
same as those exacted by Cambyses, when he was
crown-prince, from a certain Iddin-Nebo, to whom he
had lent money through the agency of his secretary,
receiving a house as security for the debt.

In some instances the slave was merely the confidential agent of his master, to whom therefore all or
most of the profits went.   Thus a deed dated in the
ninth year of Cyrus describes a field situated opposite
the gate of Zamama at Babylon, which had been assigned by "the judges" to a lady named Ê-Saggil-
belit, and afterward mortgaged by her to a slave of
Itti-Merodach-baladhu, one of the members of the
Egibi firm.   The lady, however, still wanted money,
and accordingly proposed to Itti-Merodach-baladhu
that if he would make her a "present" of 10 shekels
she would hand over to him her title-deeds.   This
was done, and the field passed into the possession of

Itti-Merodach-baladhu, with whom the mortgage had really been contracted.

In spite of the privileges possessed by the Babylonian slave, he was nevertheless a chattel, like the rest of his master's property. He could constitute the dowry of a wife, could take the place of interest on a debt or of the debt itself, and could be hired out to another, the wages he earned going into the pocket of his master. In the age of Khammurabi we find two brothers hiring the services of two slaves, one of whom belonged to their father and the other to their mother, for ten days. The slaves were wanted for harvest work, and it was agreed that a *gur* (or 180 *qas*) of grain should be paid them. This, of course, ultimately went to their owners. In the reign of Cambyses a man and his wife, having borrowed 80 shekels, gave a slave as security for the repayment of the loan; the terms of the contract are the same as if the security had been a house. On another occasion a slave is security for only part of a debt which amounted to a maneh and twenty shekels, interest being paid upon the shekels. His service was regarded as equivalent to the interest upon the maneh.

When a slave was sold the seller guaranteed that he was not disobedient, that he had not been adopted by a free citizen, that there was no prior claim to him, and that he had not been impressed into the royal service, or, in the case of female slaves, been a concubine of the king. Purchasers had to be on their guard on all these points. Strict honesty was not always the rule in the Babylonian commercial world, and a case which came before the judges in the early part of the reign of Nabonidos shows that ladies were capable of sharp practice as well as men. The judicial record states that a certain "Belit-litu gave the following evidence before the judges of Nabonidos, King of Babylon: 'In the month Ab, in the first year of Nergal-sharezer, King of Babylon, I sold my slave, Bazuzu, for thirty-five shekels of silver to Nebo-akhi-iddin, the son of Sulâ, the descendant of Egibi; he has pretended that I owed him a debt, and so has not paid me the money. The judges heard the charge, and caused Nebo-akhi-iddin to be summoned and to appear before them. Nebo-akhi-iddin produced the contract which he had made with Belit-litu; he proved that she had received the money and convinced the judges. And Ziria, Nebo-sum-lisir and Edillu gave (further) evidence before the judges that Belit-litu, their mother, had received the silver. The judges deliberated and condemned Belit-litu to (pay) fifty-five shekels (by way of fine), the highest fine that could be inflicted on her, and then gave it to Nebo-akhi-iddin.'"

The prices fetched by slaves varied naturally. We have seen that in the Abrahamic age 20 shekels (£3) were given for a white slave from the North, the same price as that for which Joseph was sold. In the reign of Ammi-zadok 4½ shekels only were paid for a female slave. In later times prices were considerably higher, though under Nebuchadnezzar we hear of a slave given as part of a dowry who was valued at 30 shekels, and of a female slave and her infant child whose cost was only 19 shekels. In the first year of Nergal-sharezer a slave-merchant of

Harran sold three slaves for 45 shekels, while a little later 32 shekels were given for a female slave. The same sum was given for a slave who was advanced in years, while a slave girl four years of age only was sold for 19 shekels. In the sixth year of Cambyses an Egyptian and her child three months old, whom the Babylonian Iddin-Nebo had "taken, with his bow," was sold by him for 2 manehs or 120 shekels, a bond for 240 *gurs* of dates being handed over to him as security for the payment of the sum. The Egyptian, it may be noted, received a Babylonian name before being put up for auction. In the same reign we hear of 3 manehs being paid for two slaves, of a maneh for a single slave, and of 7 manehs 56 shekels for three female slaves. This would be at the rate of 2 manehs 38 shekels or £23 14s. for each. On the whole, however, the average price seems to have been about 30 shekels. This, at any rate, was the case among the Israelites, not only in the Mosaic period (Exod. xxi. 32) but also in the time of the Maccabees (II. Macc. viii. 9, 10).

The fact that slaves sometimes ran away from their masters, like Barachiel, who pretended to be a free citizen, and that in contracts for their sale their obedience is expressly guaranteed, proves that they were not always content with their lot. Indeed, it is not strange that it should have been so. They were merely chattels, subject to the caprices and tyranny of those who owned them, and their lives were as little valued as that of an ox. Thus in the fortieth year of Nebuchadnezzar a judgment was delivered that, if it could be proved by witnesses that a certain

Idikhi-ilu had murdered the slave of one of the
Arameans settled in the town of Pekod, he was to be
fined a maneh of silver ; that was all the slave's life
was worth in the eyes of the law, and even that was
paid to the master to compensate him for the loss of
his property. Sometimes the name of the slave was
changed; as we have seen, the captive Egyptian
woman received a Babylonian name, and a contract
of the time of Khammurabi, relating to the female
slave of a Babylonian lady, who had been given to
her by her husband, and who, it is stipulated, shall not
be taken from her by his sons after his death, mentions that the name of the slave had been changed.
In this case, however, the reason seems to have been
that the girl was adopted by her mistress, though the
adoption was not carried out in legal form and was
therefore technically invalid. The contract accordingly describes her by her proper name of Mutibasti,
but adds that "she is called Zabini, the daughter of
Saddasu," her mistress.

That the law should nevertheless have regarded the
slave as a person. and as such possessed of definite
rights, appears strange. But Babylonian law started
from the principle of individual responsibility and
individual possession of property, and since the slave
was a human being and could, moreover, hold property of his own, it necessarily seemed to place him
more and more on a footing of equality with the free-
born citizen. The causes which brought about the
legal emancipation of women worked in the same direction in favor of the slave. Hence the power he had
of purchasing his freedom out of his own earnings and

of being adopted into a citizen's family. Hence, too, the claim of the law to interfere between the slave-owner and his property.

A slave, in fact, could even act as a witness in court, his testimony being put on the same legal level as that of a native Babylonian. He could also be a party to a suit. Thus we find a slave called Nergal-ritsua, in the tenth year of Nabonidos, bringing a suit for the recovery of stolen property. He had been intrusted by his master with the conveyance of 480 *gur* of fruit to the ships of a Syrian, named Baal-nathan, who undertook to carry it to Babylon, and to be responsible for loss. On the way part of the fruit was stolen, and Baal-nathan, instead of replacing it, absconded, but was soon caught. The slave accordingly appeared against him, and the five judges before whom the case was brought gave a verdict in his favor.

A slave could even own another slave. In the twenty-seventh year of Nebuchadnezzar, for example, the porter of the temple of the Sun-god at Sippara, who was "the slave of Nebo-baladh-yulid," purchased a female slave for two-thirds of a shekel (2s.). The amount was small, but the purchaser did not possess so much at the moment, and credit was consequently allowed him. The list of witnesses to the contract is headed by a slave.

The condition of the slave in Assyria was much what it was in Babylonia. The laws and customs of Assyria were modelled after those of Babylonia, whence, indeed, most of them had been derived. But there was one cause of difference between the two

countries which affected the character of slavery.
Assyria was a military power, and the greater part
of its slaves, therefore, were captives taken in war.
In Babylonia, on the contrary, the majority had been
born in the country, and between them and their
masters there was thus a bond of union and sympathy
which could not exist between the foreign captive
and his conqueror. In the northern kingdom slavery
must have been harsher.

Slaves, moreover, apparently fetched higher prices
there, probably on account of their foreign origin.
They cost on the average as much as a maneh (£9)
each. A contract, dated in 645 B.C., states that one
maneh and a half was given for a single female slave.
One of the contracting parties was a Syrian, and an
Aramaic docket is accordingly attached to the deed,
while among the witnesses to it we find Ammâ, "the
Aramean secretary." Ammâ means a native of the
land of Ammo, where Pethor was situated. About
the same time 3 manehs, "according to the standard
of Carchemis," were paid for a family of five slaves,
which included two children. Under Esar-haddon a
slave was bought for five-sixths of a maneh, or 50
shekels, and in the same year Hoshea, an Israelite,
with his two wives and four children, was sold for 3
manehs. With these prices it is instructive to compare the sum of 43 shekels given for a female slave
in Babylonia only four years later.

As a specimen of an Assyrian contract for the sale
of slaves we may take one which was made in 709
B.C., thirteen years after the fall of Samaria, and
which is noticeable on account of the Israelitish

names which it contains: "The seal of Dagon-
melech," we read, "the owner of the slaves who are
sold. Imannu, the woman U——, and Melchior, in
all three persons, have been approved by Summa-
ilâni, the bear-hunter from Kasarin, and he has
bought them from Dagon-melech for three manehs
of silver, according to the standard of Carchemish.
The money has been fully paid; the slaves have
been marked and taken. There shall be no reclama-
tion, lawsuit, or complaints. Whoever hereafter shall
at any time rise up and bring an action, whether it
be Dagon-melech or his brother or his nephew or
any one else belonging to him or a person in authority, and shall bring an action and charges against
Summa-ilâni, his son, or his grandson, shall pay 10
manehs of silver, or 1 maneh of gold (£140), to the
goddess Istar of Arbela. The money brings an
interest of 10 (*i.e.*, 60) per cent. to its possessors;
but if an action or complaint is brought it shall not
be touched by the seller. In the presence of Addâ
the secretary, Akhiramu the secretary, Pekah the
governor of the city, Nadab-Yahu (Nadabiah) the
bear-hunter, Bel-kullim-anni, Ben-dikiri, Dhem-Istar,
and Tabnî the secretary, who has drawn up the deed
of contract." The date is the 20th of Ab, or August,
709 B.C.

The slaves are sold at a maneh each, and bear
Syrian names. Addâ, " the man of Hadad," and Ben-
dikiri are also Syrian; on the other hand, Ahiram,
Pekah, and Nadabiah are Israelitish. It is interesting to find them appearing as free citizens of Assyria,
one of them being even governor of a city. It serves

to show why the tribes of Northern Israel so readily
mingled with the populations among whom they were
transported ; the exiles in Assyria were less harshly
treated than those in Babylonia, and they had no
memories of a temple and its services, no strong
religious feeling, to prevent them from being absorbed by the older inhabitants of their new homes.

In Assyria, as in Babylonia, parents could sell their
children, brothers their sisters, though we do not
know under what circumstances this was allowed by
the law. The sale of a sister by her brother for half
a maneh, which has already been referred to, took
place at Nineveh in 668 B.C. In the contract the
brother is called "the owner of his sister," and any
infringement of the agreement was to be punished
by a fine of "10 silver manehs, or 1 maneh of gold,"
to the treasury of the temple of Ninip at Calah.
About fifteen years later the services of a female
slave "as long as she lived" were given in payment
of a debt, one of the witnesses to the deed being
Yavanni "the Greek." Ninip of Calah received
slaves as well as fines for the violation of contracts
relating to the sale of them ; about 645 B.C., for instance, we find four men giving one to the service of
the god. Among the titles of the god is that of "the
lord of workmen ; " and it is therefore possible that
he was regarded as in a special way the patron of
the slave-trader.

It seems to have been illegal to sell the mother
without the children, at all events as long as they
were young. In the old Sumerian code of laws it
was already laid down that if children were born to

slaves whom their owner had sold while still reserving
the power of repurchasing them, he could nevertheless not buy them back unless he bought the children
at the same time at the rate of one and a half shekels
each. The contracts show that this law continued in
force down to the latest days of Babylonian independence. Thus the Egyptian woman who was sold in
the sixth year of Cambyses was put up to auction
along with her child. We may gather also that it
was not customary to separate the husband and wife.[1]
When the Israelite Hoshea, for instance, was put up
for sale in Assyria in the reign of Esar-haddon, both
his wives as well as his children were bought by the
purchaser along with him.   It may be noted that
the slave was "marked," or "tattooed," after purchase, like the Babylonian cattle.   This served a
double purpose; it indicated his owner and identified
him if he tried to run away.

In a country where slaves were so numerous the
wages of the free workmen were necessarily low.
There were, however, two classes of free workmen,
the skilled artisan and the agricultural laborer.   The
agricultural character of the Babylonian state, and the
fact that so many of the peasantry possessed land of
their own, prevented the agriculturist from sinking
into that condition of serfdom and degradation which
the existence of slavery would otherwise have
brought about.   Moreover, the flocks and cattle were
tended by Bedâwin and Arameans, who were proud

---

[1] We hear, however, of a " little girl of six years of age " being
sold for 17 shekels in the thirteenth year of Nabonidos, but she was
doubtless an orphan.

of their freedom and independence, like the Bedâwin of modern Egypt. In spite, therefore, of the fact that so much of the labor of the country was performed by slaves, agriculture was in high esteem and the free agriculturist was held in honor. Tradition told how Sargon of Akkad, the hero of ancient Babylonia, had been brought up by Akki the irrigator, and had himself been a gardener, while the god Tammuz, the bridegroom of Istar, had tended sheep. Indeed, one of the oldest titles of the Babylonian kings had been that of "shepherd."

At the same time there was a tendency for the free laborer to degenerate into a serf, attached to the soil of the farm on which he and his forefathers had been settled for centuries. A contract dated in the first year of Cyrus is an illustration of the fact. It records the lease of a farm near Sippara, which belonged to the temple of the Sun-god, and was let to a private individual by the chief priest and the civil governor of the temple. The farm contained 60 *gur* of arable land, and the lease of it included "12 oxen, 8 peasants, 3 iron plough-shares, 4 axes, and sufficient grain for sowing and for the support of the peasants and the cattle." Here the peasants are let along with the land, and presumably would have been sold with it had the farm been purchased instead of being let. They were, in fact, irremovable from the soil on which they had been born. It must, however, be remembered that the farm was the property of a temple, and it is possible that serfdom was confined to land which had been consecrated to the gods. In that case the Babylonian serfs would have corresponded with the Hebrew Nethinim, and might have been originally prisoners of war.

We learn some details of early agricultural life in Babylonia from the fragments of an old Sumerian work on farming which formed one of the text-books in the Babylonian schools. Passages were extracted from it and translated into Semitic for the use of the students, and difficult words and expressions were noted and explained. The book seems to have resembled the " Works and Days " of the Greek poet Hesiod, except that it was not in verse. We gather from it that the agricultural year began, not with Nisan, or March, but with Tisri, or September, like the Jewish civil year; at all events, it was then that the tenure of the farmer began and that his contract was drawn up with the landlord. It was then, too, after the harvest, that he took possession of the land, paying his tax to the government, repairing or making the fences, and ploughing the soil.

His tenure was of various kinds. Sometimes he undertook to farm the land, paying half the produce of it to the landlord or his agent and providing the farming implements, the seeds, and the manure himself. Sometimes the farm was worked on a co-operative system, the owner of the land and the tenant-farmer entering into partnership with one another and dividing everything into equal shares. In this case the landlord was required to furnish carts, oxen, and seeds. At other times the tenant received only a percentage of the profits—a third, a fourth, a fifth, or a tenth, according to agreement. He had also to pay the *esrâ* or tithe.

The most common form of tenure seems to have been that in which a third of the produce went to the lessor. Two-thirds of the rent, paid either in dates or in their monetary equivalent, was delivered to the landlord on the last day of the eighth month, Marchesvan, where the dates had been gathered and had been laid out to dry. By the terms of the lease the tenant was called upon to keep the farm buildings in order, and even to erect them if they did not exist. His own house was separate from that in which the farm-servants lived, and it was surrounded by a garden, planted for the most part with date-palms. If the farm-buildings were not built or were not kept in proper repair a fine was imposed upon him, which in the case quoted by the writer of the agricultural work was 10 shekels, or 30s. The tenant was furthermore expected to pay the laborers their wages, and the landlord had the power of dismissing him if the terms of the contract were not fulfilled.

The laborers were partly slaves, partly freemen, the freemen hiring themselves out at so much a month. A contract of the age of Khammurabi, for instance, states that a certain Uḥaru, had thus hired himself out for thirty days for half a shekel of silver, or 1s. 6d., but he had to offer a guarantee that he would not leave his master's service before the expiration of the month. In other cases it was a slave whose services were hired from his owner; thus, in a document from Sippara, of the same age as the preceding, we read: "Rimmon-bani hires Sumi-izitim as a laborer for his brother, for three months, at a wage of one shekel and a half, 3 measures of grain and $1\frac{1}{2}$ qa of oil. There

shall be no withdrawal from the agreement. Ibni-
A-murru and Sikni-Ea have confirmed it. Rimmon-
bani hires the laborer in the presence of Abum-ilu
(A'bimael), the son of Ibni-Samas, Ilisu-ibni, the son
of Igas-Rimmon, and Arad-Bel, the son of Akhuwam.
(Dated) the first day of Sivan." The wages evidently
went to the slave, so that he was practically in the
position of a free laborer.

When we come down to a later period, we find in
contract, dated at the end of the second year of
a Cyrus, Bunene-sar-uzur, "the son of Sum-yukin,"
hired, as a servant for a year, "from the month
Nisan to the month Adar," for 3 shekels of silver.
These were paid beforehand to a third person, and
the payment was duly witnessed and registered.
Bunene-sar-uzur was not a slave, though 9 shillings
does not seem much as wages for a whole year.
However, three years later only 1 pi, or about 50
quarts of meal, were given for a month's supply of
food to some men who were digging a canal. The
hours of work doubtless lasted from sunrise to sunset, though we have a curious document of the Macedonian period, dated in the reign of Seleucus II., in
which certain persons sell the wages they receive for
work done in a temple during the "sixth part" of a
day. The sum demanded was as much as 65 shekels.

The Aramean Bedâwin, who acted as shepherds,
or cattle-drovers, probably received better wages
than the native Babylonians. They were less numerous and were in more request; moreover, it was necessary that they should be trustworthy. The herds and
flocks were left in their charge for weeks together, on

the west bank of the Euphrates, out of sight of the cultivated fields of Babylonia and exposed to the attacks of marauders from the desert. Early Babylonian documents give long lists of the herdsmen and shepherds, and of the number of sheep or oxen for which they were responsible, and which were the property of some wealthy landowner. In the seventeenth year of Nabonidos, five of the shepherds received one shekel and a half of silver, as well as a *gur*, or about 250 quarts, of grain from the royal granary.

Some of the songs have been preserved to us with which the Babylonian laborer beguiled his work in the fields. They probably formed part of the treatise on agriculture which has already been described ; at any rate, we owe their preservation to the educational text-books, in which they have been embodied, along with Semitic translations of the original Sumerian text. Here is one which the peasants sang to the oxen as they returned from the field :

> My knees are marching,
> My feet are not resting ;
> Taking no thought,
> Drive me home.

In a similar strain the ploughman encouraged his team with the words :

> A heifer am I,
> To the mule I am yoked.
> Where is the cart ?
> Go, look for grass ;
> It is high, it is high !

Or again, the oxen, while threshing, would be addressed with the refrain:

> Before the oxen,
> As they walk,
> Thresh out the grain.

Ploughing, harrowing, sowing, reaping, and threshing constituted the chief events of the agricultural year. The winters were not cold, and the Babylonian peasant was consequently not obliged to spend a part of the year indoors shivering over a fire. In fact fuel was scarce in the country; few trees were grown in it except the palm, and the fruit of the palm was too valuable to allow it to be cut down. When the ordinary occupations of the farmer had come to an end, he was expected to look after his farm buildings and fences, to build walls and clean out the ditches.

The ditches, indeed, were more important in Babylonia than in most other parts of the world. Irrigation was as necessary as in Egypt, though for a different reason. The Chaldean plain had originally been a marsh, and it required constant supervision to prevent it from being once more inundated by the waters and made uninhabitable. The embankments which hindered the overflow of the Euphrates and Tigris and kept them within carefully regulated channels, the canals which carried off the surplus water and distributed it over the country, needed continual attention. Each year, after the rains of the winter, the banks had to be strengthened or re-made and the beds of the canals cleared out. The irrigator, moreover, was perpetually at work; the rainy season did not last long, and during the rest of the year the land was dependent on the water supplied by the rivers and canals. Irrigation, therefore, formed a large and important part of the farmers' work, and the bucket of the irrigator must have been constantly swinging. Without the irrigator the labors of the farmer would have been of little avail.

CHAPTER V

MANNERS AND CUSTOMS

BABYLONIA was a land of bricks. Stone was not found nearer than the mountains of Elam on the one side or the desert plains of Northern Arabia on the other. Clay, on the contrary, was plentiful, and the art of making bricks and building a house by means of them must have been invented by the first settlers in the country. The bricks were dried in the sun, the heat of which was sufficient to harden them. The clay was further bound together by being mixed with chopped reeds, though the use of the latter was not universal, at all events in the earlier times. In the later days of Babylonian history, however, they were generally employed, and we learn from the contracts that a bed of reeds grown for the sake of the brickmakers' trade was by no means an unprofitable investment. Either clay or bitumen took the place of mortar; the bitumen was procured from Hit or from the Kurdish hills, where there are still springs of naphtha; after the conquest of Canaan it may have been brought from the neighborhood of the Dead Sea. Some scholars have thought that this is referred to by Gudea, the priest-king of Lagas (2700 B.C.).

The employment of brick had a very direct effect upon the character of Babylonian architecture. Thick walls, supported by buttresses and devoid of sculpture, were necessitated by it. The buildings of Babylonia were externally plain and flat; masses of brick were piled up in the form of towers or else built into long lines of wall of unbroken monotony. The roofs were made of the stems of palm-trees, which rested on the stems of other palm-trees, where the space between one brick wall and another was too great to be safely spanned. The upright stems became columns, which were imitated first in brick and then in stone. Babylonia was thus the birthplace of columnar architecture, and in the course of centuries columns of almost every conceivable shape and kind came to be invented. Sometimes they were made to stand on the backs of animals, sometimes the animal formed the capital. The column which rested against the wall passed into a brick pilaster, and this again assumed various forms.

The monotony of the wall itself was disguised in different ways. The pilaster served to break it, and the walls of the early Chaldean temples are accordingly often broken up into a series of recessed panels, the sides of which are formed by square pilasters. Clay cones were also inserted in the wall and brilliantly colored, the colors being arranged in patterns. But the most common form of decoration was where the wall was covered with painted stucco. This, indeed, was the ordinary mode of ornamenting the internal walls of a building; a sort of dado ran round the lower part of them painted with the figures

of men and animals, while the upper part was left in
plain colors or decorated only with rosettes and similar designs. Ezekiel[1] refers to the figures of the
Chaldeans portrayed in vermilion on the walls of their
palaces, and the composite creatures of Babylonian
mythology who were believed to represent the first
imperfect attempts at creation were depicted on the
walls of the temple of Bel.

Among the tablets which have been found at Tello
are plans of the houses of the age of Sargon of
Akkad. The plans are for the most part drawn to
scale, and the length and breadth of the rooms
and courts contained in them are given. The rooms
opened one into the other, and along one side of a
house there usually ran a passage. One of the houses,
for example, of which we have a plan, contained five
rooms on the ground floor, two of which were the
length of the house. The dimensions of the second
of·these is described as being 8 cubits in breadth
and 1 *gardu* in length. The *gardu* was probably
equivalent to 18 cubits or about 30 feet. In another
case the plan is that of the house of the high priest
of Lagas, and at the back of it the number of slaves
living in it is stated as well as the number of workmen employed to build it. It was built, we are told,
in the year when Naram-Sin, the son of Sargon,
made the pavement of the temples of Bel at Nippur
and of Istar at Nin-unu.

The temple and house were alike erected on a platform of brick or earth. This was rendered necessary
by the marshy soil of Babylonia and the inundations

[1] Xxiii. 14.

to which it was exposed. The houses, indeed, generally found the platform already prepared for them by the ruins of the buildings which had previously stood on the same spot. Sun-dried brick quickly disintegrates, and a deserted house soon became a mound of dirt. In this way the villages and towns of Babylonia gradually rose in height, forming a *tel* or mound on which the houses of a later age could be erected.

In contrast to Babylonia the younger kingdom of Assyria was a land of stone. But the culture of Assyria was derived from Babylonia, and the architectural fashions of Babylonia were accordingly followed even when stone took the place of brick. The platform, which was as necessary in Babylonia as it was unnecessary in Assyria, was nevertheless servilely copied, and palaces and temples were piled upon it like those of the Babylonians. The ornamentation of the Babylonian walls was imitated in stone, the rooms being adorned with a sculptured dado, the bas-reliefs of which were painted in bright colors. Even the fantastic shapes of the Babylonian columns were reproduced in stone. Brick, too, was largely used; in fact, the stone served for the most part merely as a facing, to ornament rather than strengthen the walls.

The Babylonian princes had themselves set the example of employing stone for the sake of decoration. Stone was fetched for the purpose from the most distant regions, regardless of cost. Gudea, the priest-king of Lagas, imported limestone from the Lebanon and from Samalum, near the Gulf of Antioch, while the statues which adorned his palace, and are now in the Louvre, are carved out of diorite from the Peninsula of Sinai. The diorite doubtless came by sea, but the blocks of hewn stone that were brought from "the land of the Amorites" must have been conveyed overland.

Even more precious materials than stone were used for decorative purposes. Gold and silver, bronze and ivory, lapis-lazuli and colored glass, ornamented the cornices and other parts of the interior of the palace. Gudea tells us that he had sent to the deserts which bordered on Egypt for gold-dust and acacia-wood, to Arabia for copper, and to Mount Amanus for beams of cedar. The elephant was still hunted on the banks of the Euphrates near the city of Carchemish, and lapis-lazuli was furnished by the mountains of Persia.

A garden was planted by the side of the house. The Babylonians were an agricultural people, and even the cities were full of the gardens attached to the houses of all who could afford to have them. Originally the garden was little more than a grove of palms. But herbs and vegetables soon began to be grown in it, and as habits of luxury increased, exotic trees and shrubs were transplanted to it and flowers were cultivated for the sake of their scent. Tiglath-pileser I. of Assyria tells us how he had "taken and planted in the gardens of his country cedars" and other trees "from the lands he had conquered, which none of the kings his predecessors had ever planted before," and how he had "brought rare vines which did not exist in Assyria and had cultivated them in the land of Assyria." At a later date Sennacherib laid out a pleasure-garden or "paradise" by the side of the palace he erected, filling it with cypresses and other trees as well as fragrant plants, and digging a lake in the midst of it by means of which it could be watered. One of the bas-reliefs in the palace of As-sur-bani-pal represents the King and Queen dining in the royal garden under the shadow of its palms, while an attendant drives away the insects with a fan. The Assyrians did but imitate their Babylonian neighbors, and in the gardens of Nineveh we must see many copies of the gardens that had been laid out in Babylonia long ages before. The very word "paradise," which in the Persian age came to signify a pleasure-park, was of Babylonian origin. It is given in the exercise-book of a Babylonian school-boy as the name of a mythical locality, and an etymological pun attempts to derive it from the name of the god Esu.

It was, of course, only the houses of the rich and noble which were artistically furnished or provided with a garden. The poorer classes lived in mud huts of conical form, which seldom contained more than one or two rooms. Air and light were admitted through the door or through small apertures in the walls. In the better class of houses, on the other hand, the windows were of large size, and were placed near the ceiling. The air was excluded by means of curtains which were drawn across them when the weather was cold or when it was necessary to keep out the sunlight. The houses, moreover, consisted of more than one story, the upper stories being approached by a flight of steps which were open to the air. They were usually built against one

of the sides of a central court, around which the
rooms were ranged, the rooms on the upper floors
communicating with one another by means of a covered corridor, or else by doors leading from one chamber to the other. The apartments of the women
were separate from those of the men, and the servants
slept either on the ground-floor or in an outbuilding
of their own.

The furniture, even of the palaces, was scanty from
a modern point of view. The floor was covered with
rugs, for the manufacture of which Babylonia was
famous, and chairs, couches, and tables were placed
here and there. The furniture was artistic in form ;
a seal-cylinder, of the age of Ur-Bau, King of Ur, the
older contemporary of Gudea, represents a chair, the
feet of which have been carved into the likeness of
those of oxen. If we may judge from Egyptian anal-
ogies the material of which they were formed would
have been ivory. The Assyrian furniture of later days
doubtless followed older Babylonian models, and we
can gain from it some idea of what they must have
been like. The chairs were of various kinds. Some
had backs and arms, some were mere stools. The
seats of many were so high that a footstool was required by those who used them. The employment
of the footstool must go back to a considerable antiquity. since we find some of the Tel-el-Amarna cor-
respondents in the fourteenth century before our era
comparing themselves to the footstool of the King.
Chairs and stools alike were furnished with cushions
which were covered with embroidered tapestries. So
also were the couches and bedsteads used by the

wealthier classes. The poor contented themselves with a single mattress laid upon the floor, and since everyone slept in the clothes he had worn during the day, rising in the morning was not a difficult task.

The tables had four legs, and the wood of which they were composed was often inlaid with ivory. Wood inlaid with ivory and other precious materials was also employed for the chairs and sofas. Tripods of bronze, moreover, stood in different parts of the room, and vases of water or wine were placed upon them. Fragments of some of them have been found in the ruins of Nineveh, and they are represented in early Babylonian seals. The feet of the tripod were artistically shaped to resemble the feet of oxen, the clinched human hand, or some similar design. At meals the tripod stood beside the table on which the dishes were laid. Those who eat sat on chairs in the earlier period, but in later times the fashion grew up, for the men at any rate, to recline on a couch. Assur-bani-pal, for example, is thus represented, while the Queen sits beside him on a lofty chair. Perhaps the difference in manners is an illustration of the greater conservatism of women who adhere to customs which have been discarded by the men.

Vases of stone and earthenware, of bronze, gold, and silver, were plentifully in use. A vase of silver mounted on a bronze pedestal with four feet, which was dedicated to his god by one of the high-priests of Lagas, has been found at Tello, and stone bowls, inscribed with the name of Gudea, and closely resembling similar bowls from the early Egyptian tombs, have also been disinterred there. A vase of Egyptian

alabaster, discovered by the French excavators in
Babylonia, but subsequently lost in the Tigris, bore
upon it an inscription stating it to have been part of
the spoil obtained by Naram-Sin, the son of Sargon
of Akkad, from his conquest of the Sinaitic peninsula. In Assyrian days the vases were frequently of
porcelain or glass ; when these were first introduced
is still unknown. Various articles of furniture are
mentioned in the later contracts. Under Nabonidos,
7 shekels, or 21 shillings, were given for a copper kettle and cup, the kettle weighing 16 manehs (or 42
pounds troy) and the cup 2 manehs (5 pounds 7
ounces troy). These were left, it may be noted, in
the safe-keeping of a slave, and were bought by a
lady. At a later date, in the third year of Cambyses,
as much as 4 manehs 9 shekels, or £36 7s., were paid
for a large copper jug and *qulla*, which was probably
of the same form as the *qullas* of modern Egypt.
The female slave who seems to have started an inn
in the sixth year of Cambyses provided herself with
five bedsteads, ten chairs, three dishes, one ward-
robe (?), three shears, one iron shovel, one syphon,
one wine-decanter, one chain (?), one brazier, and
other objects which cannot as yet be identified. The
brazier was probably a Babylonian invention. At all
events we find it used in Judah after contact with
Assyria had introduced the habits of the farther East
among the Jews (Jer. xxxvi. 22), like the gnomon or
sun-dial of Ahaz (Is. xxxviii. 8), which was also of
Babylonian origin (Herod., ii., 109). The gnomon
seems to have consisted of a column, the shadow of
which was thrown on a flight of twelve steps repre-

senting the twelve double hours into which the diurnal revolutions of the earth were divided and which thus indicated the time of day.

What the chairs, tables, footstools, and couches were like may be seen from the Assyrian bas-reliefs. They were highly artistic in design and character, and were of various shapes. The tables or stands sometimes had the form of camp-stools, sometimes were three-legged, but more usually they were furnished with four legs, which occasionally were placed on a sort of platform or stand. At times they were provided with shelves. Special stands with shelves were also made for holding vases, though large jars were often made to stand on tripods.

If we may judge from the old lists of clothing that have come down to us, the Babylonians must have been fond of variety in dress. The names of an immense number of different kinds of dress are given, and the monuments show that fashions changed from time to time. Thus the earliest remains of Chaldean art exhibit three successive changes in the head-dress, and similar changes are to be noticed in the dress of the Assyrian kings as it is represented in the bas-reliefs.

To the last, however, the principal constituents of Babylonian dress remained the same. There were a hat or head-dress, a tunic or shirt, and a long robe which reached to the ankles, to which in cold weather was added a cloak. The hat or cap was made of some thick substance like felt and was sometimes quilted. The Babylonian King Merodach-nadin-akhi (1100 B.C.) is represented in a square cap which is

ornamented with a row of feathers; below these is a
band of rosettes. The Assyrian King generally wore
a lofty tiara; this was a survival of the tiara of the
early Babylonians. Above his head was carried a
parasol to protect him from the sun; but the use of
the parasol was confined to the upper classes, if not
to the royal family alone.

The tunic was of linen, or more often of wool,
which was manufactured in Babylonia on a large
scale. It reached half-way down the knees and was
fastened round the waist by a girdle. Under it a
second tunic or vest was sometimes worn in cold
weather. Drawers were seldom used, though in the
time of the second Assyrian empire the cavalry and
heavy-armed bowmen wore tightly fitting drawers of
plaited leather, but the custom was probably introduced from the north. A bilingual vocabulary, however, gives a Sumerian word for this article of dress,
which may therefore have been occasionally adopted
in pre-Semitic days.

The long robe was usually sleeveless and ornamented with a fringe. It opened in front, and in
walking allowed the left leg to be seen. The girdle was
often tied around it instead of round the tunic. The
Assyrian King is sometimes represented as wearing a
sort of richly embroidered cape over the robe. The
cape or cloak, however, was specially characteristic
of the Babylonians, as the Assyrians found it incon-
venient in war or active exercise, and accordingly preferred to discard it. Most of them wore it only on
state occasions or when in full dress.

The feet were shod with sandals, though the Babylonians, as a rule, went barefoot. So also did the lower classes among the Assyrians, as well as a portion of the army. The sandals were attached to the foot by leather thongs, and the heel was protected by a cap. The boot, however, was introduced from the colder regions of the north before the twelfth century B.C. At all events, Merodach-nadin-akhi is depicted as wearing soft leather shoes, and Sennacherib adopted a similar foot-covering. This was laced in front like the high-laced boots with which the Assyrian cavalry were provided toward the end of the reign of Tiglath-pileser III.

The priest was distinguished by a curiously flounced dress, made perhaps of a species of muslin, which descended to the feet, and is often pictured on the early seals. Over his shoulders was flung a goat's skin, the symbol of his office, like the leopard's skin worn by the priests in Egypt.

In the early Babylonian period the dress of all classes was naturally much more simple than that of a later date. The poor were contented with a short kilt, the King and his family with a long one. One of the early rulers of Lagas, for instance, is represented as wearing only a skull-cap and a kilt which reaches nearly to the ankles. It was under the Semitic empire of Sargon of Akkad that the long robe seems first to have become common. But it was worn over the left shoulder only, and as the tunic was not yet introduced into ordinary use, the right shoulder was left bare. Even Naram-Sin, the conqueror of Sinai, is depicted as clad in this simple costume in a bas-relief found near Diarbekr. The robe is quilted,

and on the King's head is a conical cap of felt. The
statues of the age of Gudea also show no sign of the
tunic. The development out of the kilt must belong
to a later age.

The costume of the women does not appear to
have differed much from that of the men. Both
alike adopted the long robe. But representations
of women are unfortunately rare. The Queen of As-
surbani-pal is dressed in a long, sleeveless robe,
over which is a fringed frock reaching to the knees,
and over this again a light cape, also fringed and embroidered with rosettes. This may, therefore, be
regarded as the official dress of a grand lady in the
closing days of the Assyrian empire.

Both men and women were fond of jewelry, and
adorned themselves with rings, bracelets, ear-rings,
and necklaces. The women also wore anklets, like
many of the Oriental women of to-day. The men
carried a stick in the street, and all who could afford
it had a small engraved cylinder of stone attached to
the wrist by a ring which passed through an orifice
in the cylinder. The cylinder served the purpose of
a seal, and was constantly required in business transactions. No deed was valid without the seal or mark
of the contracting parties; when either of them was
too poor to possess a seal, a nail-mark was impressed
upon the clay of the contract tablet, and a note added
stating to whom it was that the mark belonged.

The seal-cylinder was a Babylonian invention.
In a land where there were no stones every pebble was of value, and the Babylonians accordingly
became expert gem-cutters at a very early period.

Gem-cutting, in fact, was a highly developed art among them, and the seal-cylinder of Ibni-sarru, the librarian of Sargon of Akkad, which is now in a private collection in Paris, is one of the most beautiful specimens of the art that has ever been produced. The pebble was cut in a cylindrical shape, and various figures were engraved upon it. The favorite design was that of a god or goddess to whom the owner of the seal is being introduced by a priest; sometimes the King takes the place of the deity, at other times it is the adventures of Gilgames, the hero of the great Chaldean Epic, that are represented upon the stone. The design is usually accompanied by a few lines of inscription, giving the name of the owner of the seal, as well as that of his father, and stating of what god or King he was "the servant." The seals were often kept in stock by their makers, a blank space being left for the inscription, which was to be engraved upon them as soon as they had found a purchaser. Hence it is that at times the names have never been filled in.

The style and pattern of the cylinder changed in the course of centuries, as well as the favorite materials of which it was made. Under the dynasty of Ur, which preceded that of Khammurabi, for instance, hæmatite was more especially in vogue; in the age of Nebuchadnezzar crystal became fashionable. At one period, moreover, or among the artists of a particular local school, the representation of a human sacrifice was common. Between the inscription on the cylinder, however, and the subjects engraved upon it there is seldom, if ever, any connection, except

when a portrait is given of the god or King of whom
the owner calls himself the servant.

A hole was drilled through the length of the cylinder, and through this a string was passed. Instead
of the string a rod of metal or ivory was often employed; this was fixed in a frame of gold or bronze,
and the cylinder was thus able to turn upon it.
When the seal was used it was rolled over the soft
clay, leaving an indelible impression behind. Among
the objects found at Tello are balls of clay, which
were attached to papyrus documents, like the seals
of mediæval deeds, and sealed with the cylinders of
the post-masters of Sargon and Naram-Sin. Above
the seal comes the address, in one case to Naram-Sin,
in another to the high-priest of Lagas. It is evident that a postal system had already been established between Lagas and Agade or Akkad, the capital of Sargon's empire. The impressions show that
the seals must have been very beautiful specimens of
workmanship. They all belonged to high officials;
one to Dada, "the seer of the palace," another to the
high-priest of Lagas himself.

Great attention was paid to the hair of the head
and beard. But this was more especially the case
among the Semites, who were a bearded race. The
older Sumerian population had but little hair upon
the face, and to the last the typical Babylonian
was distinguished from the Assyrian by the greater
absence of beard. The result was that while the
Semite encouraged his hair to grow, the Sumerian
shaved it except in the case of old men. Most of
the Sumerian heads which have been discovered in

the excavations of Tello have smooth faces and
shorn heads. The figures represented on the so-
called Stela of the Vultures, one of the earliest examples of Chaldean art, are without beards, and on the
early seal-cylinders the gods alone, as a rule, are
permitted to wear them. We are reminded of the
Egyptian custom which forbade the beard except to
the King and the god. The barber, in fact, occupied
an important position in ancient Babylonia, and the
old Sumerian code of laws enjoins that a son who
denies his father shall be shorn and sold as a slave.

With the rise of Semitic supremacy, however,
there is a great change. Naram-Sin, in the bas-
relief of Diarbekr, wears beard and whiskers and
mustache like the Assyrians of a later day, and like
them also his hair is artificially curled, though to a
lesser extent. The same long beard also distin-
guishes Khammurabi in a piece of sculpture in
which he is entitled "the king of the land of the
Amorites." The gods, too, now assume a mustache
as well as a beard and take upon them a Semitic
character.

The use of cosmetics must have become widely
spread, and many of the small stone vases in which
they were kept and which have been found on the
sites of Babylonian cities were doubtless intended
for the hair-dresser. The oil that was poured upon
the hair made it bright and shining and it was worn
long whether it grew on the head or on the face.
The Babylonians had long been known as "the people
of the black heads," perhaps in contrast to the fairer
inhabitants of the Kurdish mountains to the north,

and the black hair, frizzled and curled, was now allowed to be visible. The working classes bound it with a simple fillet; the wealthier members of society protected it with caps and tiaras. But all alike were proud of it; the days were past when a beardless race had held rule in Western Asia.

CHAPTER VI

BABYLONIA, as we have seen, was essentially an industrial country. In spite of its agricultural basis and the vast army of slaves with which it was filled, it was essentially a land of trades and manufactures. Its manufacturing fame was remembered into classical days. One of the rooms in the palace of Nero was hung with Babylonian tapestries, which had cost four millions of sesterces, or more than £32,000, and Cato, it is said, sold a Babylonian mantle because it was too costly and splendid for a Roman to wear. The wool of which the cloths and rugs of Babylonia were made was derived from the flocks which fed on the banks of the Euphrates, and a large body of artisans was employed in weaving it into tapestries and curtains, robes and carpets. They were woven in bright and vari-colored patterns; the figures of men and animals were depicted upon them and the bas-relief or fresco could be replaced upon the wall by a picture in tapestry. The dyes were mainly vegetable, though the kermes or cochineal-insect, out of which the precious scarlet dye was extracted, was brought from the neighborhood of the Indus. So at least Ktesias states in the age of the Persian empire; and

since teak was found by Mr. Taylor among the ruins
of Ur, it is probable that intercourse with the western
coast of India went back to an early date. Indeed
an old bilingual list of clothing gives *sindhu* as the
name of a material which is explained to be "vegetable wool;" in this we must see the cotton which in
the classical epoch was imported from the island of
Tylos, in the Persian Gulf, but which, as its name
declares, must have originally been "the Indian"
plant.

The looms and weavers of Babylonia are, as is
natural, repeatedly referred to in the contracts, many
of which, moreover, relate to the sale and purchase
of wool. One of them even shows us Belshazzar, the
son and heir-apparent of the King Nabonidos, as a
wool-merchant on a considerable scale. "The sum
of 20 manehs for wool," it says, "the property of
Belshazzar, the son of the king, which has been
handed over to Iddin-Merodach, the son of Basa, the
son of Nur-Sin, through the agency of Nebo-zabit,
the servant of the house of Belshazzar, the son of the
king, and the secretaries of the son of the king. In
the month Adar (February) of the eleventh year (of
Nabonidos) the debtor shall pay the money, 20
manehs. The house of —— the Persian and all the
property of Iddin-Merodach in town and country
shall be the security of Belshazzar, the son of the
king, until he shall pay in full the money aforesaid.
The money which shall (meanwhile) accrue upon (the
wool) he shall pay as interest." Then follow the names
of five witnesses and a priest, as well as the date and
the place of registration. This was Babylon, and the

priest, Bel-akhi-iddin, who helped to witness the deed
was a brother of Nabonidos and consequently the
uncle of Belshazzar.

The weight of the wool that was sold is unfortunately not stated. But considering that 20 manehs,
or £180, was paid for it, there must have been a considerable amount of it. In the reign of Cambyses
the amount of wool needed for the robe of the image
of the Sun-goddess Â was as much as 5 manehs 5
shekels in weight. Wealthy land-owners kept large
flocks of sheep, chiefly for the sake of their wool.
Their prices varied greatly. Thus in the fourth year
of Nabonidos, 6 shekels, or 18s., were given for a
sheep, while in the thirteenth year of the same King,
18 sheep fetched only 35 shekels, or less than 6s., each.
In the first year of Cyrus, 6 lambs were sold for $8\frac{1}{4}$
shekels, and 5 other lambs for $7\frac{1}{4}$ shekels, while 1
sheep cost only one shekel and a quarter; in his sixth
year the price of a single sheep had risen to 4 shekels
(12s.). Under Cambyses we find sheep selling for 7
and $7\frac{1}{4}$ shekels apiece. In the eighth year of Nabonidos, 100 sheep were sold for 50 shekels after they
had been slaughtered; it is clear, therefore, that the
dead animal was considered less valuable than the
living one.

On the other hand, sheep cost a good deal to feed
when the grazing season was over, and they had to be
fed " in the stall." A document dated in the seventh
year of Cyrus states that 32 sheep required each day
1 pi 28 qas (or about 95 quarts) of grain, while 160
full-grown animals consumed daily 4 pi 16 qas, or more
than 240 quarts. In the reign of Cambyses 1 pi 4

qas of fodder were needed daily for 20 old sheep, 100
qas for 100 younger sheep, and the same amount
also for 200 lambs. At this time 2 *pi* of grain cost
6½ shekels; consequently the cost of keeping the 20
old sheep alone was about 10s 6d. a day. To this
had to be added the wages of the shepherds, who were
free Bedâwin. Hence, it is not wonderful that the
owner demanded 7 shekels, or 21s., for the sheep he
had to sell.

In the *Edin* or "field," however, their keep came
to but little. The pasturage was common property,
and it was only the wages of the Aramean shepherds
who looked after the flock which involved an outlay.
The five shepherds who, in the tenth year of Nabonidos, were paid for their services by the overseer of
the royal flocks in the town of Ruzabu received 30
shekels of silver and a *gur* of grain. The *gur* contained 180 *qas*, and since in the first year of Cyrus
two men received 2 *pi* 30 *qas*, or 102 *qas*, of grain for
their support during a month of thirty days, we may,
perhaps, infer that the wages were intended to cover
the third part of a month. In this case each man
would have been paid at the rate of 9 shekels, or 37s.,
a month. It is, however, possible that the wages
were really intended for the full month. The ancient
Greeks considered a quart of wheat a sufficient daily
allowance for a grown man, and 180 *qas* would mean
about 1⅔ of a quart a day for each man.

We may gather from a contract dated the 5th of
Sivan in the eighteenth year of Darius that it was
not customary to pay for any sheep that were sold
until they had been driven into the city, the cost of

doing so being included in the prize. The contract
is as follows: "One hundred sheep of the house of
Akhabtum, the mother of Sa-Bel-iddin, the servant of
Bel-sunu, that have been sold to La-Bel, the son of
Khabdiya, on the 10th day of the month Ab in
the eighteenth year of Darius the king: The sheep,
200 in number, must be brought into Babylon and
delivered to Supêsu, the servant of Sa-Bel-iddin. If
15 manehs of silver are not paid for the sheep on the
10th of Ab, they must be paid on 20th of the month. If
the money, amounting to 15 manehs, is not paid, then
interest shall be paid according to this agreement at
the rate of one shekel for each maneh per month."
Then come the names of eight witnesses and a priest,
the date, and the place of registration, which was a
town called Tsikhu.

The contract is interesting from several points
of view. The sheep, it will be seen, belonged to a
woman, and not to her son, who was "the servant" of
a Babylonian gentleman and had another "servant"
who acted as his agent at Babylon. The father of
the purchaser of the sheep bears the Hebrew name
of 'Abdî, which is transcribed into Babylonian in the
usual fashion, and the name of the purchaser himself,
which may be translated "(There is) no Bel," may
imply that he was a Jew. Akhabtum and her son
were doubtless Arameans, and it is noticeable that
the latter is termed a "servant" and not a "slave."

Before entering the city an *octroi* duty had to be
paid upon the sheep as upon other produce of the
country. The custom-house was at the gate, and the
duty is accordingly called "gate-money" in the con-

tracts. In front of the gate was an open space, the
rêbit, such as may still be seen at the entrance to
an Oriental town, and which was used as a market-
place. The *rêbit* of Nineveh lay on the north
side of the city, in the direction where Sargon built
his palace, the ruins of which are now known as
Khorsabad. But besides the market-place outside
the walls there were also open spaces inside them
where markets could be held and sheep and cattle
sold. Babylon, it would seem, was full of such public
"squares," and so, too, was Nineveh. The *suqi* or
"streets" led into them, long, narrow lanes through
which a chariot or cart could be driven with difficulty. Here and there, however, there were streets
of a broader and better character, called *suli*, which
originally denoted the raised and paved ascents
which led to a temple. It was along these that the
religious processions were conducted, and the King
and his generals passed over them in triumph after
a victory. One of these main streets, called Â-ibur-
sabu, intersected Babylon; it was constructed of
brick by Nebuchadnezzar, paved with large slabs of
stone, and raised to a considerable height. It started
from the principal gate of the city, and after passing
Ê-Saggil, the great temple of Bel-Merodach, was carried as far as the sanctuary of Istar. When Assur-
bani-pal's army captured Babylon, after a long siege,
the "mercy-seats" of the gods and the paved roads
were "cleansed" by order of the Assyrian King and
the advice of "the prophets," while the ordinary
streets and lanes were left to themselves.

It was in these latter streets, however, that the

shops and bazaars were situated.   Here the trade of
the country was carried on in shops which possessed
no windows, but were sheltered from the sun by
awnings that were stretched across the street.   Behind the shops were magazines and store-houses, as
well as the rooms in which the larger industries, like
that of weaving, were carried on.   The scavengers of
the streets were probably dogs.   As early as the
time of Khammurabi, however, there were officers
termed *rabiani*, whose duty it was to look after " the
city, the walls, and the streets."   The streets, moreover, had separate names.

Here and there " beer-houses " were to be found,
answering to the public-houses of to-day, as well as
regular inns.   The beer-houses are not infrequently
alluded to in the texts, and a deed relating to the
purchase of a house in Sippara, of the age of Khammurabi, mentions one that was in a sort of underground cellar, like some of the beer-houses of modern
Germany.

Sippara lay on both sides of the Euphrates, like
Babylon, and its two halves were probably connected
by a pontoon-bridge, as we know was the case at
Babylon.   Tolls were levied for passing over the
latter, and probably also for passing under it in boats.
At all events a document translated by Mr. Pinches
shows that the quay-duties were paid into the same
department of the government as the tolls derived
from the bridge.   The document, which is dated in
the twenty-sixth year of Darius, is so interesting
that it may be quoted in full : " The revenue derived
from the bridge and the quays, and the guard-house,

which is under the control of Guzanu, the captain of
Babylon, of which Sirku, the son of Iddinâ, has
charge, besides the amount derived from the tolls
levied at the bridge of Guzanu, the captain of Babylon, of which Muranu, the son of Nebo-kin-abli,
and Nebo-bullidhsu, the son of Guzanu, have charge :
Kharitsanu and Iqubu (Jacob) and Nergal-ibni are
the watchmen of the bridge.   Sirku, the son of
Iddinâ, the son of Egibi, and Muranu, the son of
Nebo-kin-abli, the son of the watchman of the pontoon, have paid to Bel-asûa, the son of Nergal-yubal-
lidh, the son of Mudammiq-Rimmon, and Ubaru, the
son of Bel-akhi-erba, the son of the watchman of the
pontoon, as dues for a month, 15 shekels of white
silver, in one-shekel pieces and coined.   Bel-asûa and
Ubaru shall guard the ships which are moored under
the bridge.   Muranu and his trustees, Bel-asûa and
Ubaru, shall not pay the money derived from the
tolls levied at the bridge, which is due each month
from Sirku in the absence of the latter.   All the
traffic over the bridge shall be reported by Bel asûa
and Ubaru to Sirku and the watchmen of the bridge."

House-property was valuable, especially if it included shops.   As far back as the reign of Eri-Aku,
or Arisch, 2¼ shekels were given for one which stood
on a piece of ground only 1⅝ *sar* in area, the *sar*, if
Dr. Reisner is right, being the eighteen-hundredths
part of the *feddan* or acre.   In the twentieth year of
Assur-bani-pal, just after a war which had desolated
Babylonia, a house was sold in the provincial town
of Erech for 75 shekels (£11 5s.), and in the beginning
of the reign of Nabonidos a carpenter's shop in Bor-

sippa, the suburb of Babylon, which was not more than
7 rods, 5 cubits, and 18 inches in length, was bought
by the agent of the Syrian Ben-Hadad-nathan and
his wife for 11½ manehs, or £103 10s. On the other
hand, in the reign of Cambyses, we hear of smaller
prices being given for houses in Babylon, 4½ manehs
for a house with a piece of land attached to it, and 2
manehs for one that had been the joint property of
a man and his wife; while in the ninth year of Nergal-sharezer a house was sold for only 52½ shekels.

Houses, however, were more frequently let than
sold. Already, in the age of Khammurabi, we have
the record of the lease of a house for eight years.
At a later date contracts relating to the renting of
houses are numerous. Thus in the sixth year of
Cyrus a house was let at a yearly rent of 10 shekels,
part of which was to be paid at the beginning of the
year and the rest in the middle of it. The tenant
was to renew the fences when necessary and repair
all dilapidations. He was also expected to send a
present to his landlord thrice a year in the months of
Nisan, Tammuz, and Kisleu. Other houses in Babylon in the Persian age were let at yearly rents of 5
shekels, 5½ shekels, 7½ shekels, 9 shekels, 15 shekels,
20 shekels, 23 shekels, and 35 shekels, the leases
running for two, three, five, and more years. The
tenant usually undertook to keep the property in
repair and to make good all dilapidations. Loss in
case of fire or other accidents also fell upon him.
Most of the houses seem to have been inhabited by
single families; but there were tenements or flats as
well, the rent of which was naturally lower than that

of a whole house. Thus we find a woman paying
only 2 shekels, or 6s., a year for a tenement in the
reign of Cambyses.

Any violation of the lease involved a fine, the
amount of which was stated in the contract. A
house, for instance, was let at Babylon in the first
year of Cambyses for 5 shekels a year, the rent to
be paid in two halves "at the beginning and in the
middle of the year." In this case a breach of the
contract was to be punished by a fine of 10 shekels,
or double the amount of the rent. In other cases
the fine was as much as a maneh of silver.

Occasionally the primitive custom was retained of
paying the rent in kind instead of in coin. We even
hear of "six overcoats" being taken in lieu of rent.
The rent of a house might also take the place of
interest upon a loan, and the property be handed
over to the creditor as security for a debt. Thus in
the second and last year of the reign of Evil-Merodach (560 B.C.), and on the fourth of the month Ab,
the following agreement was drawn up at Babylon :
"Four manehs of silver belonging to Nadin-akhi, the
son of Nur-Ea, the son of Masdukku, received from
Sapik-zeri, the son of Merodach-nazir, the son of
Liu-Merodach. The house of Sapik-zeri, which is
in the street Khuburru, and adjoins the houses of
Rimut-Bel, the son of Zeriya, the son of the Egyptian,
and of Zeriya, the son of Bel-edheru, shall be handed
over as security to Nadin-akhi. No rent shall be
paid for it, and no interest demanded for the debt.
Sapik-zeri shall have it for three years. He must
renew the fences and repair all injuries to the walls.

At the end of the three years Sapik-zeri sha.. repay
the money—namely, four manehs—to Nadin-akhi, and
the latter shall vacate the house. The rent of the
warehouse of the eunuch is included, of which Sapik-
zeri enjoys the use. Whatever doors Nadin-akhi may
have added to the house during his tenancy he shall
take away." Then come the names of three witnesses,
one of them being the brother of the creditor, as well
as of the clerk who drew up the document.

A few years later, in the fifth year of Nabonidos
(551 B.C.), we find the heir-apparent, Belshazzar, receiving house-property on similar terms. "The house
of Nebo-akhi-iddin, the son of Sula, the son of Egibi,"
we read, "which adjoins the house of Bel-iddin, the
son of Birrut, the son of the life-guardsman, is handed over for three years as security for a loan of 1½ manehs to Nebo-kin-akhi, the agent of Belshazzar, the
son of the king, on the following conditions: no rent
shall be paid for the house, and no interest paid
on the debt. The tenant shall renew the fences and
make good all dilapidations. At the end of three
years the 1½ manehs shall be paid by Nebo-akhi-iddin
to Nebo-kin-akhi, and Nebo-kin-akhi shall vacate
the house of Nebo-akhi-iddin. Witnessed by Kabtiya, the son of Talnea, the son of Egibi; by Sapik-
zeri, the son of Nergal-yukin, the son of Sin-karab-
seme; by Nebo-zer-ibni, the son of Ardia, and the
clerk, Bel-akhi-iqisa, the son of Nebo-balasu-ikbi, at
Babylon, the 21st day of Nisam (March) and the fifth
year of Nabonidos, King of Babylon."

This was not the only transaction of the kind in
which Belshazzar appears, though it is true that his

business was carried on by means of agents. Six
years later we have another contract relating to his
commercial dealings which has already been quoted
above.[1] It illustrates the intensely commercial spirit
of the Babylonians, and we may form some idea of
the high estimation in which trade was held when we
see the eldest son of the reigning King acting as a
wool merchant and carrying on business like an ordinary merchant.

An interesting document, drawn up in Babylonia
in the eleventh year of Sargon (710 B.C.), shortly after
the overthrow of Merodach-Baladan, contains an account of a lawsuit which resulted from the purchase
of two "ruined houses" in Dur-ilu, a town on the
frontier of Elam. They had been purchased by a
certain Nebo-liu for 85 shekels, with the intention of
pulling them down and erecting new buildings on the
site. In order to pay the purchase money Nebo-liu
demanded back from "Bel-usatu, the son of Ipunu,"
the sum of 30 shekels which he claimed to have lent
him. Bel-usatu at first denied the claim, and the
matter was brought into court. There judgment was
given in favor of the plaintiff, and the defendant was
ordered to pay him 45 shekels, 15, or half the amount
claimed, being for "costs." Thereupon Bel-usatu
proposed:

" 'Instead of the money, take my houses, which are
in the town of Der.' The title-deeds of these houses,
the longer side of which was bounded to the east by
the house of Bea, the son of Sulâ, and to the west by
the entrance to a field which partly belonged to the

[1] P.

property, while the shorter side was bounded to the
north by the house of Ittabsi, and to the south by the
house of Likimmâ, were signed and sealed by Nebo-
usatu, who pledged himself not to retract the deed or
make any subsequent claim, and they were then handed
over to Nebo-liu." The troubles of the latter, however, were not yet at an end. "Ilu-rabu-bel-sanât,
Sennacherib, and Labasu, the sons of Rakhaz the
[priest] of the great god, said to Nebo-liu: 'Seventy-
three shekels of your money you have received from
our father. Give us, therefore, 50 shekels and we
will deliver to you the house and its garden which
belonged to our father.' The house, which was fit
only to be pulled down and rebuilt, along with a
grove of forty date-bearing palms, was situated on the
bank of the canal of Dûtu in Dur-ilu, its longer side
adjoining on the north the house of Edheru, the son
of Baniya, the priest of Â, and on the south the canal
of Dûtu, while its shorter side was bounded on the
east by the house of Nergal-epus, and on the west by
the street Mutaqutu. Nebo-liu agreed, and looked
out and gave Rakhaz and his sons 50 shekels of silver,
together with an overcoat and two shekels by way
of a *bakshish* to bind the bargain, the whole amounting to 52 shekels, paid in full." The custom of adding
a *bakshish* or "present" to the purchase-money at the
conclusion of a bargain is still characteristic of the
East. Other examples of it are met with in the Babylonian contracts, and prove how immemorially old it is.
Thus in the second year of Darius, when the three
sons of a "smith" sold a house near the Gate of Zamama, at Babylon, to the grandson of another "smith,"

besides the purchase money for the house, which amounted to 67½ shekels, the buyer gave in addition a *bakshish* of 2½ shekels (7s. 6d.) as well as "a dress for the lady of the house." Three shekels were further given as " a present " for sealing the deed. So too, the negotiations for the sale of some land in the second year of Evil-Merodach were accompanied by a *bakshish* of 5 shekels.

Lawsuits connected with the sale or lease of houses do not seem to have been uncommon. One of the documents which have come down to us from the ancient records of Babylon is a list of "the judges before whom Sapik-zeri, the son of Zirutu, and Baladhu, the son of Nasikatum, the slave of the secretary for the Marshlands," were called upon to appear in a suit relating to "the house and deed which Zirutu, the father of Sapik-zeri, had sealed and given to Baladhu," who had afterward handed both of them over to Sapik-zeri. Among the judges we find the governor of the Marshlands, who acted as president, the sub-governor, the mayor of Erech, the priest of Ur, and one of the governors of the district " beyond " the Euphrates. The list is dated the 6th of Nisan or March, in the seventeenth year of Nebuchadnezzar.

The value of land was proportionate to that of house-property. In the early days of Babylonia its value was fixed by the amount of grain that could be grown upon it, and it was accordingly in grain that the owner was paid by the purchaser or lessee. Gradually, however, a metal currency took the place of the grain, and in the later age of Babylonian history even the rent was but rarely paid in kind. We

learn from a lawsuit decided in the reign of Samsu-
iluna, the son of Khammurabi, that it was customary
for an estate to be "paced round" by the *rabia-
num* or "magistrates" of the city. The ceremony
was equivalent to "beating the bounds" of a parish
in modern England, and it is probable that it was
performed every year. Such at least is the custom
in Egypt, where the limits of a piece of property are
measured and fixed annually. The Babylonian document in which the custom is referred to relates to a
dispute about a plantation of acacias which grew in
the neighborhood of the modern Tel Sifr. The magistrates, before whom it was brought, are described
as looking after not only the city but also "the walls
and streets," from which we may gather that municipal commissioners already existed in the Babylonian towns. The plaintiff made oath before them
over the copper libation-bowl of the god of Boun-
daries, which thus took the place of the Bible in an
English court of law.

A few years later, in the reign of Ammi-zadok,
three men rented a field for three years on terms of
partnership, agreeing to give the owner during the
first two years 1 *gur* of grain upon each *feddan* or
acre. The whole of the third harvest was to go to
the lessees, and the partners were to divide the crop
in equal shares "on the day of the harvest."

When we come to the twelfth century B.C., however, the maneh and shekel have been substituted
for the crops of the field. Thus we hear of 704 shekels and a fraction being paid for a field which was
calculated to produce 3 *gur* of corn, and of 110 shek-

els being given for another estate which contained
a grove of date-palms and on which 2 *gur* of grain
were sown. How much grain could be grown on a
piece of land we can gather from the official reports
of the cadastral survey. In the sixth year of Cyrus,
for example, the following report was drawn up of
the "measurement of a corn-field and of the corn in
the ear" belonging to a Babylonian taxpayer:

Length of the field on its longer side.	Length of the field on its narrower side.	Amount of crop.	Value in grain.	Tenant.
1020	395	13 *gur*, 18 *qa*, of which 1 *gur*, 18 *qa*, are destroyed.	Each 25 *gur* is worth 300 *gur* of grain.	Nadbanu.
540	550	10 *gur*, 2 *pi*, 29 *qa*, of which 3 *g u r* are destroyed.	Each 20 *gur* is worth 130 *gur*.	Arad-Bel.

The cadastral survey for purposes of taxation went
back to an early period of Babylonian history. It
was already at work in the age of Sargon of Akkad.
The survey of the district or principality of Lagas
(now Tello) which was drawn up in that remote
epoch of history is in our hands, and is interesting on
account of its reference to a "governor" of the land
of the Amorites, or Canaan, who bears the Canaanitish name of Urimelech. The survey states that the
district in question contained 39,694 acres, 1,325 *sar*,
as well as 17 large towns and 8 subdivisions.

Another cadastral survey from Lagas, but of the
period of Khammurabi, which has recently been published by Dr. Scheil, tells us that the towns on the

lower banks of "the canal of Lagas" had to pay the
treasury each year 35⅝ shekels of silver according to
the assessment of the tax-collector Sin-mustal.   One
of the towns was that of the Aramean tribe of Pekod.   Another is called the town of the Brewers,
and another is described as "the Copper-Foundry."
Most of the towns were assessed at half a shekel,
though there were some which had to pay a shekel
and more.   Among the latter was the town of Ninâ,
which gave its name to the more famous Nineveh on
the Tigris.   The surveyor, it should be added, was
an important personage in Babylonian society, and
the contract tablets of the second Babylonian empire
not unfrequently mention him.

Assyria, like Babylonia, has yielded us a good
many deeds relating to the sale and lease of houses
and landed estate.   We can estimate from them the
average value of house-property in Nineveh in the
time of the second Assyrian empire, when the wealth
of the Eastern world was being poured into it and
the Assyrian kings were striving to divert the trade
of Phœnicia into their own hands.   Thus, in 694 B.C.,
a house with two doors was sold for 3 manehs 20
shekels, and two years subsequently another which
adjoined it was purchased for 1 maneh "according
to the royal standard."   The contract for the sale is
a good example of what an Assyrian deed of sale in
such a case was like.   " The nail-marks of Sar-ludari,
Akhassuru, and Amat-Suhla, the wife of Bel-suri, the
official, the son of the priest, and owner of the house
which is sold.   The house, which is in thorough repair, with its woodwork, doors, and court, situated in

the city of Nineveh and adjoining the houses of Mannu-ki-akhi and Ilu-ittiya and the street *Sipru*, has been negotiated for by Zil-Assur, the Egyptian secretary. He has bought it for 1 maneh of silver according to the royal standard from Sar-ludari, Ak-hassuru, and Amat-Suhla, the wife of Bel-duri. The money has been paid in full, and the house received as bought. Withdrawal from the contract, lawsuits, and claims are hereby excluded. Whoever hereafter at any time, whether these men or others, shall bring an action and claims against Zil-Assur, shall be fined 10 manehs of silver. Witnessed by Susanqu-khatna-nis, Murmaza the official, Rasuh the sailor, Nebo-dur-uzur the champion, Murmaza the naval captain, Sin-sar-uzur, and Zidqa (Zedekiah). The sixteenth of Sivan during the year of office of Zaza, the gov-ernor of Arpad (692 B.C.)." It is noticeable that the first witness has a Syrian name.

One of the characteristics of the Assyrian deeds is that so few of the parties who appear in them are able to write their names. Nail-marks take the place of seals even in the case of persons who hold official positions and who are shown by the contracts to have been men of property. In this respect Assyria offers a striking contrast to Babylonia, where "the nail-mark" seldom makes its appearance. Closely connected with this inability to write is the absence of the seal-cylinder, which was part of the ordinary dress of the Babylonian gentleman. In the Assyrian contracts, on the other hand, it is conspicuous by its absence. The use of it in Assyria was an imitation of Babylonian manners, and was confined for the

most part to the scribes and higher official class, who
had received a literary education.

Land in Assyria was measured by homers rather
than by *feddans* or acres as in Babylonia. In 674
B.C. an estate of 35 homers, in the town of Sairi,
was sold for 5 manehs, any infringement of the
contract being punished by a fine of 10 manehs of
silver or one of gold, to be paid into the treasury of
the temple of Istar. We learn incidentally from
this that the value of gold to silver at the time was
as one to ten. Five years previously 6 homers of
land in another small Assyrian town had been let at
an annual rent of 1 maneh of silver "according to
the standard of Carchemish." In the reign of Assur-
bani-pal a homer of corn-land was rented for six
years for 10 shekels a year. The land was calculated
to produce 9 *qas* of grain, and at the end of the first
three years it was stipulated that there should be a
rotation of crops. About the same time two fields,
enclosing an area of 3⅔ homers, were leased by a certain Rimu-ana-Bel of Beth-Abimelech, whose father's
name, Yatanael, shows that he was of Syrian origin.
The steward of "the son of a king" took them for
six years at an annual rent of 12 shekels. One of
the fields contained a well, and yielded 15 *qas* of
grain to each homer. It is stated in the contract
that the fields had no mortgage upon them, and that
the lessee had a right to the whole of the crop which
they produced.

It was not in Assyria only that plots of ground
could be leased and sold in accordance with the provisions of Assyrian law. Conquest had brought

landed property into the hands of Assyrians in other
parts of the Eastern world, and it could be put up
to auction at Nineveh, where the proprietors lived.
About 660 B.C., for instance, a considerable estate was
thus sold in the oasis of Singara, in the centre of Mesopotamia. It lay within the precincts of the temple
of Istar, and contained a grove of 1,000 young palms.
It included, moreover, a field of 2 homers planted
with terebinths, house - property extending over 6
homers, a house with a corn-field attached to it, and
another house which stood in the grove of Yarkhu,
the Moon-god. The whole was sold for 4 shekels
of silver " according to the standard of Carchemish,"
and the penalty for any infringement of the contract
was again to be the payment of a maneh of gold
(£90) to the treasury of the goddess Istar. When
one of the parties to the contract was of Aramean descent, it was usual to add an explanatory docket in
Aramaic to the deed of sale. Indeed, this seems to
have been sometimes done even where there were no
Arameans in the case, so thoroughly had Aramaic
become the common language of trade. Thus in the
year of Sennacherib's office as eponym (687 B.C.) we
hear of the sale of three shops in Nineveh on the
part of a certain Dain-kurban, whose name is written
in Aramaic letters on the outer envelope of the deed
of sale. Thirty shekels were paid for them, and a
fine of 10 manehs imposed upon anyone who should
attempt to invalidate the sale. The shops seem to
have been situated in the Syrian quarter of the city,
as we are told that they were opposite the tenement
of Nakharau, "the man of Nahor."

It will have been noticed how frequently it is stated that a " plantation " or grove of palms is attached to the house or field which is rented and sold. In Babylonia, in fact, an estate was not considered complete without its garden, which almost invariably included a clump of palms. The date-palm was the staple of the country. It was almost the only tree which grew there, and it grew in marvellous abundance. Stem, leaves, and fruit were all alike turned to use. The columns and roofing-beams of the temples and houses were made of its stem, which was also employed for bonding the brick walls of the cities. Its fibres were twisted into ropes, its leaves woven into baskets. The fruit it bore was utilized in many ways. Sometimes the dates were eaten fresh, at other times they were dried and exported to foreign lands; out of some of them wine was made, out of others a rich and luscious sugar. It was little wonder that the Babylonian regarded the palm as the best gift that Nature had bestowed upon him. Palmland necessarily fetched a higher price than cornland, and we may conclude, from a contract of the third year of Cyrus, that its valuation was seven and one-half times greater.

Trade partnerships were common, and even commercial companies were not unknown. The great banking and money-lending firm which was known in Babylonia under the name of its founder, Egibi, and from which so many of the contract-tablets have been derived, was an example of the latter. It lasted through several generations and seems to have been but little affected by the political revolutions and changes which took place at Babylon. It saw the rise and fall of the empire of Nebuchadnezzar, and flourished quite as much under the Persian as under the native kings.

As far back as the reign of Samsu-iluna we find women entering into partnership with men for business purposes on a footing of absolute equality. A certain Amat-Samas, for instance, a devotee of the Sun-god, did so with two men in order to trade with a maneh of silver which had been borrowed from the treasury of the god. It was stipulated in the deed which was indentured when the partnership was made that in case of disagreement the capital and interest accruing from it were to be divided in equal shares among the three partners.

In the later Babylonian period the contract was drawn up in much the same form, though with a little more detail. In the report of a trial dated the eighth day of Sebat or January, in the eighteenth year of Nebuchadnezzar II., we have the following reference to one that had been made twenty-one years before: "A partnership was entered into between Nebo-yukin-abla and his son Nebo-bel-sunu on the one side and Musezib-Bel on the other, which lasted from the eighteenth year of Nabopolassar, King of Babylon, to the eighteenth year of Nebuchadnezzar. The contract was produced before the judge of the judges. Fifty shekels of silver were adjudged to Nebo-bel-sunu and his father Nebo-yukin-abla. No further agreement or partnership exists between the two parties. . . . They have ended their contract with one another. All former obligations in their names are rescinded."

One of the latest Babylonian deeds of partnership
that have come down to us is dated in the fifth year
of Xerxes. It begins with the statement that " Bel-
edheru, son of Nergal-edheru and Ribâta, son of Kasmani, have entered into partnership with one another,
contributing severally toward it 2½ manehs of silver
in stamped shekel-pieces and half a maneh of silver,
also in stamped shekel-pieces. Whatever profits Ribâta shall make on the capital—namely, the 3 manehs
in stamped shekel-pieces—whether in town or country, [he shall divide with] Bel-edheru proportionally
to the share of the latter in the business. When the
partnership is dissolved he shall repay to Bel-edheru
the [2½] manehs contributed by him. Ribâta, son
of Kasmani, undertakes all responsibility for the
money." Then come the names of six witnesses.

Money, however, was not the only subject of a
deed of partnership. Houses and other property
could be bought and sold and traded with in common. Thus we hear of Itti-Merodach-baladh, the
grandson of " the Egyptian," and Merodach-sapik-
zeri starting as partners with a capital of 5 manehs
of silver and 130 empty barrels, two slaves acting as
agents, and on another occasion we find it stipulated
that " 200 barrels full of good beer, 20 empty barrels,
10 cups and saucers, 90 gur of dates in the storehouse, 15 gur of chickpease (?), and 14 sheep, besides
the profits from the shop and whatever else Bel-sunu
has accumulated, shall be shared between him " and
his partner.

The partners usually contributed in equal parts to
the business, and the profits were divided equally

among them.   Where this was not the case, provision
was made for a proportionate distribution of profit
and loss.   All profits were included, whether made,
to use the language of Babylonian law, "in town or
country."   The partnership was generally entered into
for a fixed term of years, but could be terminated
sooner by death or by agreement.   One of the partners
could be represented by an agent, who was often a
slave; in some instances we hear of the wife taking
the place of her husband or other relation during his
absence from home.   Thus in a deed dated in the
second year of Nergal-sharezer (559 B.C.) we read:
"As long as Pani-Nebo-dhemi, the brother of Ili-
qanua, does not return from his travels, Burasu, the
wife of Ili-qanua, shall share in the business of Ili-
qanua, in the place of Pani-Nebo-dhemi. When Pani-
Nebo-dhemi returns she shall leave Ili-qanua and hand
over the share to Pani-Nebo-dhemi."   As one of the
witnesses to the document is a "minister of the king"
who bears the Syrian name of Salammanu, or Solomon the son of Baal-tammuh, it is possible that Pani-
Nebo-dhemi was a Syrian merchant whose business
obliged him to reside in a foreign country.

That partnerships in Babylonia were originally
made for the sake of foreign trade seems probable
from the name given to them.   This is *kharran*, which
properly means a "road" or "caravan."   The earliest
partners in trade would have been the members of a
caravan, who clubbed together to travel and traffic in
foreign lands and to defend themselves in common
from the perils of the journey.

The products of the Babylonian looms must have

been among the first objects which were thus sent
abroad. We have already described the extensive
industry which brought wealth into Babylonia and
made it from the earliest ages the centre of the trade
in rugs and tapestries, cloths and clothing. A large
part of the industrial population of the country must
have been employed in the factories and shops where
the woven and embroidered fabrics were produced
and made ready for sale. Long lists exist giving the
names of the various articles of dress which were thus
manufactured. The goodly " Babylonish garment "
carried off by Achan from the sack of Jericho was but
one of the many which found their way each year
to the shores of the Mediterranean.

The trades of the dyer and the fuller flourished by
the side of that of the cloth-maker. So, too, did the
trade of the tanner, leather being much used and
finely worked. The shoes of the Babylonian ladies
were famous; and the saddles of the horses were
made with elaborate care.

The smith, too, occupied an honorable position.
In the earlier period of Babylonian history, gold, silver, copper, and bronze were the metals which he
manufactured into arms, utensils, and ornaments.
At a later date, however, iron also came to be exten-
sively used, though probably not before the sixteenth
century B.C. The use of bronze, moreover, does not
seem to go back much beyond the age of Sargon of
Akkad; at all events, the oldest metal tools and
weapons found at Tello are of copper, without any
admixture of tin. Most of the copper came from the
mines of the Sinaitic Peninsula, though the metal

was also found in Cyprus, to which reference appears
to be made in the annals of Sargon. The tin was
brought from a much greater distance. Indeed, it
would seem that the nearest sources for it—at any
rate in sufficient quantities for the bronze of the Oriental world—were India and the Malayan Peninsula
on the one hand, and the southern extremity of Corn-
wall on the other. It is not surprising, therefore,
that it should have been rare and expensive, and
that consequently it was long before copper was
superseded by the harder bronze. Means, however,
were found for hardening the copper· when it was
used, and copper tools were employed to cut even the
hardest of stones.

The metal, after being melted, was run into moulds
of stone or clay. It was in this way that most of
the gold and silver ornaments were manufactured
which we see represented in the sculptures. Stone
moulds for ear-rings have been found on the site of
Nineveh, and the inscriptions contain many references to jewelry. The gold was also worked by the
hand into beaded patterns, or incised like the silver
seals, some of which have come down to us. Most
of the gold was originally brought from the north;
in the fifteenth century before our era the gold mines
in the desert on the eastern side of Egypt provided
the precious metal for the nations of Western Asia.

A document found among the records of the trading firm of Murasu at Nippur, in the fifth century B.C.,
shows that the goldsmith was required to warrant the
excellence of his work before handing it over to the
customer, and it may be presumed that the same rule

held good for other trades also. The document in question is a guarantee that an emerald has been so well set in a ring as not to drop out for twenty years, and has been translated as follows by Professor Hilprecht: " Bel-akh-iddina and Bel-sunu, the sons of Bel, and Khatin, the son of Bazuzu, have made the following declaration to Bel-nadin-sumu, the son of Murasu: As to the gold ring set with an emerald, we guarantee that for twenty years the emerald will not fall out of the ring. If it should fall out before the end of twenty years, Bel-akh-iddina [and the two others] shall pay Bel-nadin-sumu an indemnity of ten manehs of silver." Then come the names of seven witnesses and of the clerk who drew up the deed, and the artisans add their nail-marks in place of seals.

Many of the articles of daily use in the houses of the people, such as knives, tools of all kinds, bowls, dishes, and the like, were made of copper or bronze. They were, however, somewhat expensive, and as late as the reign of Cambyses we find that a copper libation-bowl and cup cost as much as 4 manehs 9 shekels, (£37 7s.), and about the same time 22 shekels (£3 3s.) were paid for two copper bowls 7½ manehs in weight. If the weight in this case were equivalent to that of the silver maneh the cost would have been nearly 4d. per ounce. It must be remembered that, as in the modern East, the workman expected the metal to be furnished by his customer; and accordingly we hear of 3 manehs of iron being given to a smith to be made into rods for bows. Three manehs of iron were also considered sufficient for the manufacture of six swords, two oboe-rings, and two

bolts. All this, of course, belongs to the age of
the second Babylonian empire, when iron had taken
the place of bronze.

The carpenter's trade is another handicraft to
which there is frequent allusion in the texts. Already, before the days of Sargon of Akkad, beams
of wood were fetched from distant lands for the temples and palaces of Chaldea. Cedar was brought
from the mountains of Amanus and Lebanon, and
other trees from Elam. The palm could be used for
purely architectural purposes, for boarding the crude
bricks of the walls together, or to serve as the rafters
of the roof, but it was unsuitable for doors or for the
wooden panels with which the chambers of the temple or palace were often lined. For such purposes
the cedar was considered best, and burnt panels of
it have been found in the sanctuary of Ingurisa at
Tello. Down to the latest days panels of wood were
valuable in Babylonia, and we find it stipulated in
the leases of houses that the lessee shall be allowed
to remove the doors he has put up at his own expense.

But the carpenter's trade was not confined to inar-
tistic work. From the earliest age of Babylonian
history he was skilled in making household furniture,
which was often of a highly artistic description. On
a seal-cylinder, now in the British Museum, the King
is represented as seated on a chair which, like those
of ancient Egypt, rested on the feet of oxen, and
similarly artistic couches and chests, inlaid with
ivory or gold, were often to be met with in the houses
of the rich. The Assyrian sculptures show to what
perfection the art of the joiner had attained at the

time when Nineveh was the mistress of the civilized
world.

The art of the stone-cutter had attained an even
higher perfection at a very remote date. Indeed,
the seal-cylinders of the time of Sargon of Akkad
display a degree of excellence and finish which was
never surpassed at any subsequent time. The same
may be said of the bas-relief of Naram-Sin discovered
at Diarbekr. The combination of realism and artistic finish displayed in it was never equalled even
by the bas-reliefs of Assyria, admirable as they are
from many points of view.

The early stone-cutters of Chaldea tried their skill
upon the hardest materials, and engraved upon them
the minutest and most delicate designs. Hæmatite
was a favorite material for the seal-cylinder; the
statues of Tello are carved out of diorite, which was
brought from the Sinaitic Peninsula, and stones of
similar hardness were manufactured into vases. That
such work should have been attempted in an age
when iron and steel were as yet unknown seems to
us astonishing. Even bronze was scarce, and the
majority of the tools employed by the workmen were
made of copper, which was artificially hardened when
in use. Emery powder or sand was also used, and
the lathe had long been known. When iron was first
introduced into the workshops of Babylonia is
doubtful. That the metal had been recognized at
a very early period is clear from the fact that in
the primitive picture-writing of the country, out of
which the cuneiform syllabary developed, it was
denoted by two characters, representing respectively

"heaven" and "metal." It would seem, therefore, that the first iron with which the inhabitants of the Babylonian plain were acquainted was of meteoric origin.

In the age of the Egyptian empire in Asia, at the beginning of the seventeenth century B.C., iron was passing into general use. Objects of iron are referred to in the inscriptions, and a couple of centuries later we hear of iron chariots among the Canaanites, and of ironsmiths in Palestine, who repair the shattered vehicles of Egyptian travellers in that country. It must have been at this time that the bronzesmith in Babylonia became transformed into an ironsmith.

Carving in ivory was another trade followed in Babylonia and Assyria. The carved ivories found on the site of Nineveh are of great beauty, and from a very early epoch ivory was used for the handles of sceptres, or for the inlaid work of wooden furniture. The "ivory couches" of Babylonia made their way to the West along with the other products of Babylonian culture, and Amos (vi. 4) denounces the wealthy nobles of Israel who "lie upon beds of ivory." Thothmes III. of Egypt, in the sixteenth century B.C., hunted the elephant on the banks of the Euphrates, not far from Carchemish, and, as late as about 1100 B.C., Tiglath-pileser I. of Assyria speaks of doing the same. In the older period of Babylonian history, therefore, the elephant would have lived on the northern frontier of Babylonian domination, and its tusks would have been carried down the Euphrates along with other articles of northern trade.

Quite as old as the trade of the carver in ivory was that of the porcelain-maker. The walls of the palaces and temples of Babylonia and Assyria were adorned with glazed and enamelled tiles on which figures and other designs were drawn in brilliant colors; they were then covered with a metallic glaze and fired. Babylonia, in fact, seems to have been the original home of the enamelled tile and therewith of the manufacture of porcelain. It was a land of clay and not of stone, and while it thus became necessary to ornament the plain mud wall of the house, the clay brick itself, when painted and protected by a glaze, was made into the best and most enduring of ornaments. The enamelled bricks of Chaldea and Assyria are among the most beautiful relics of Babylonian civilization that have survived to us, and those which adorned the Persian palace of Susa, and are now in the Museum of the Louvre, are unsurpassed by the most elaborate productions of modern skill.

Our enumeration of Babylonian trades would not be complete without mention being made of that of the brick-maker. The manufacture of bricks was indeed one of the chief industries of the country, and the brick-maker took the position which would be taken by the mason elsewhere. He erected all the buildings of Babylonia. The walls of the temples themselves were of brick. Even in Assyria the slavish imitation of Babylonian models caused brick to remain the chief building material of a kingdom where stone was plentiful and clay comparatively scarce. The brick-yards stood on the outskirts of the cities, where the ground was low and where a

thick bed of reeds grew in a pond or marsh. These
reeds were an important requisite for the brick-
maker's art; when dried they formed a bed on which
the bricks rested while they were being baked by the
sun; cut into small pieces they were mixed with the
clay in order to bind it together; and if the bricks
were burnt in a kiln the reeds were used as fuel.
They were accordingly artificially cultivated, and
fetched high prices. Thus, in the fourteenth year of
Nabonidos, we hear of 2 shekels being given for 200
bundles of reeds for building a bridge across a
canal, and a shekel for 100 bundles to be made into
torches. At the same time 55 shekels were paid for
8,000 loads of brick. The possession of a bed of
reeds added to the value of an estate, and it is, therefore, always specified in deeds relating to the sale of
property. One, situated at Sippara, was owned by a
scribe, Arad-Bel, who has drawn up several contracts,
as we learn incidentally from a document dated in
the seventh year of Cyrus, in which Ardi, the
grandson of "the brickmaker," agrees to pay two-
thirds of the bricks he makes to Arad-Bel, on condition of being allowed to manufacture them in the
reed-bed of the latter. This is described as adjoining "the reed-bed of Bel-baladan and the plantation
of the Sun-god."

The brick-maker was also a potter, and the manifold products of the potter's skill, for which Babylonia was celebrated, were manufactured in the
corner of the brick-field. Here also were made the
tablets, which were handed to the professional scribe
or the ordinary citizen to be written upon, and so take

the place of the papyrus of ancient Egypt or the paper of to-day. The brick-maker was thus not only a potter, but the provider of literary materials as well. He might even be compared with the printer of the modern world, since texts were occasionally cut in wood and so impressed upon moulds of clay, which, after being hardened, were used as stamps, by means of which the texts could be multiplied, impressions of them being mechanically reproduced on other tablets or cylinders of clay.

Another Babylonian trade which must be noticed was that of the vintner. Wine was made from dates as well as from grapes, while beer, called *sikaru*, was also manufactured, probably from some cereal grain. Mention is found of a "wine" that was made from sesame. The vine was not a native of Babylonia, but must have been introduced into it from the highlands of Armenia at a very early date, as it was known there long before the days of Sargon of Akkad. Large quantities of wine and beer were drunk in both Babylonia and Assyria, and reference has already been made to the bas-relief in which the Assyrian King, Assur-bani-pal, and his Queen are depicted drinking wine in the gardens of his palace, while the head of his vanquished foe, the King of Elam, hangs from the branch of a neighboring tree. A receipt, dated the eleventh day of Iyyar, in the first year of Nabonidos, is for the conveyance of " 75 *qas* of meal and 63 *qas* of beer for the sustenance of the artisans ; " and in the thirty-eighth year of Nebuchadnezzar 20 shekels were paid for " beer," the amount of which, however, is unfortunately not

stated. But two "large" casks of new wine cost 11
shekels, and five other smaller casks 10 shekels.
Moreover, the inventory of goods to be handed over
to the slave Khunnatu, in the sixth year of Cambyses, includes fifty casks of "good beer," which,
together with the cup with which it was drawn, was
valued at 60 shekels (£9).

Whether any grape-wine was made in Babylonia
itself was questionable ; at any rate, the greater part
of that which was drunk there was imported from
abroad, more especially from Armenia and Syria.
The wines of the Lebanon were specially prized,
the wine of Khilbunu, or Helbon, holding a chief
place among them. The wines, some of which were
described as "white," were distinguished by the
names of the localities where they were made or in
which the vines were grown, and Nebuchadnezzar
gives the following list of them : The wine of Izalla,
in Armenia; of Tuhimmu, of Zimmini, of Helbon, of
Amabanu, of the Shuhites, of Bit-Kubati, in Elam;
of Opis and of Bitati, in Armenia. To these another
list adds : "The wine reserved for the king's drinking," and the wines of Nazahzê, of Lahû, and of the
Khabur.

The wine was kept in wine-cellars, and among the
Assyrian letters that have come down to us are some
from the cellarers of the King. In one of them it is
stated that the wine received in the month Tebet had
been bottled, and that there was no room in the royal
cellars in which it could be stored. The King is
therefore asked to allow new cellars to be made.

The various trades formed guilds or corporations,

and those who wished to enter one of these had to
be apprenticed for a fixed number of years in order
to learn the craft. As we have seen, slaves could
be thus apprenticed by their owners and in this
way become members of a guild. What the exact
relation was between the slave and the free members
of a trading guild we do not know, but it is probable that the slave was regarded as the representative of his master or mistress, who accordingly became, instead of himself, the real member of the
corporation. We perhaps have a parallel in modern
England, where a person can be elected a member of
one of the "city companies," or trade guilds, without being in any way connected with the trade himself. Since women in Babylonia were able to carry
on a business, there would be no obstacle to a slave
being apprenticed to a trade by his mistress. Hence
it is that we find a Babylonian lady named Nubtâ, in
the second year of Cyrus, apprenticing a slave to a
weaver for five years. Nubtâ engaged to provide
the apprentice with clothing and 1 *qa* (nearly 2
quarts) of grain each day. As in ancient Greece a
quart of grain was considered a sufficient daily allowance for a man, the slave's allowance would seem to
have been ample. The teacher was to be heavily
fined if he failed to teach the trade, or overworked
the apprentice and so made him unable to learn it,
the fine being fixed at 6 *qas* (about 10 quarts) *per
diem.* Any infringement of the contract on either
side was further to be -visited with a penalty of 30
shekels of silver.

As 30 shekels of silver were equivalent to £4 10s.,

6 *qas* of wheat at the time when the contract was drawn up would have cost about 1s. 3d. Under Nebuchadnezzar we find 12 *qas*, or the third part of an ardeb, of sesame sold for half a shekel, which would make the cost of a single quart a little more than a penny. In the twelfth year of Nabonidos 60 shekels, or £9, were paid for 6 *gur* of sesame, and since the *gur* contained 5 ardebs, according to Dr. Oppert's calculation, the quart of sesame would have been a little less than 1½d. When we come to the reign of Cambyses we hear of 6½ shekels being paid for 2 ardebs, or about 100 quarts, of wheat; that would give 2½d. as the approximate value of a single *qa*. It would therefore have cost Nubtâ about 2½d. a day to feed a slave.

It must, however, be remembered that the price of grain varied from year to year. In years of scarcity the price rose; when the crops were plentiful it necessarily fell. To a certain extent the annual value was equalized by the large exportation of grain to foreign countries, to which reference is made in many of the contract-tablets; the institution of royal or public store-houses, moreover, called *sutummê*, tended to keep the price of it steady and uniform. Nevertheless, bad seasons sometimes occurred, and there were consequent fluctuations in prices. This was more especially the case as regards the second staple of Babylonian food and standard of value—dates. These seem to have been mostly consumed in Babylonia itself, and, though large quantities of them were accumulated in the royal storehouses, it was upon a smaller scale than in the case of the grain. Hence

we need not be surprised if we find that while in the
seventh year of Nebuchadnezzar a shekel was paid
for 1⅛ ardebs of dates, or about a halfpenny a quart,
in the thirtieth year of the same reign the price had
fallen to one-twenty-fifth of a penny per quart. A
little later, in the first year of Cambyses, 100 *gur* of
dates was valued at 2½ shekels (7s. 6d.), the *gur* containing 180 *qas*, which gives 2d. per each *qa*, and in
the second year of Cyrus a receipt for the payment of
" the workmen of the overseer " states that the following amount of dates had been given from " the royal
store-house " for their " food " during the month
Tebet : " Fifty *gur* for the 50 workmen, 10 *gur* for 10
shield-bearers, 2 *gur* for the overseer, 1 *gur* for the
chief overseer; in all, 63 *gurs* of dates." It was consequently calculated that a workman would consume
a *gur* of dates a month, the month consisting of thirty
days.

About the same period, in the first year of Cyrus,
after his conquest of Babylon, we hear of two men
receiving 2 *pi* 30 *qas* (102 *qas*) of grain for the
month Tammuz. Each man accordingly received a
little over a *qa* a day, the wage being practically the
same as that paid by Nubtâ to the slave. On the
other hand, a receipt dated in the fifteenth year of
Nabonidos is for 2 *pi* (72 *qas*) of grain, and 54 *qas*
of dates were paid to the captain of a boat for the
conveyance of mortar, to serve as " food " during the
month Tebet. As " salt and vegetables " were also
added, it is probable that the captain was expected
to share the food with his crew. A week previously
8 shekels had been given for 91 *gur* of dates owed by

the city of Pallukkatum, on the Pallacopas canal, to
the temple of Uru at Sippara, but the money was
probably paid for porterage only. At all events, five
years earlier a shekel and a quarter had been paid
for the hire of a boat which conveyed three oxen and
twenty-four sheep, the offering made by Belshazzar
"in the month Nisan to Samas and the gods of
Sippara," while 60 qas of dates were assigned to the
two boatmen for food. This would have been a qa of
dates *per diem* for each boatman, supposing the voy-
age was intended to last a month. In the ninth year
of Nabonidos 2 *gur* of dates were given to a man as
his nourishment for two months, which would have
been at the rate of 6 qas a day. In the thirty-second
year of the same reign 36 qas of dates were valued at
a shekel, or a penny a qa.

In the older period of Babylonian history prices
were reckoned in grain, and, as might be expected,
payment was made in kind rather than in coin. In
the reign of Ammi-zadok, for instance, 3 homers
24⅔ qas of oil, though valued at 20⅔ shekels of silver,
were actually bought with "white Kurdish slaves,"
it being stipulated that if the slaves were not forthcoming the purchaser would have to pay for the oil
in cash. A thousand years later, under Merodach-
nadin-akhi, cash had become the necessary medium
of exchange. A cart and harness were sold for 100
shekels, six riding-horses for 300 shekels, one "ass
from the West" for 130 shekels, one steer for 30
shekels, 34 *gur* 56 qas of grain for 137 shekels, 2
homers 40 qas of oil for 16 shekels, two long-sleeved
robes for 12 shekels, and nine shawls for 18 shekels.

From this time forward we hear no more of payment
in kind, except where wages were paid in food, or
where tithes and other offerings were made to the
temples. Though the current price of wheat continued to fix the market standard of value, business
was conducted by means of stamped money. The
shekel and the maneh were the only medium of exchange.

There are numerous materials for ascertaining the
average prices of commodities in the later days of
Babylonian history. We have already seen what
prices were given for sheep and wool, as well as the
cost of some of the articles of household use. In
the thirty-eighth year of Nebuchadnezzar 100 *gur*
of wheat were valued at only 1 maneh—that is to
say, the *qa* of wheat was worth only the hundredth
part of a shilling—while at the same time the price of
dates was exactly one-half that amount. On the
other hand, in the fourth year of Cambyses 72 *qas*
of sesame were sold at Sippara for 6½ shekels,
or 19s. 6d. This would make the cereal worth
approximately 1½d. a quart, the same price as that
at which it was sold in the twelfth year of Nabonidos. In the second year of Nergal-sharezer twenty-
one strings of onions fetched as much as 10 shekels,
and a year later 96 shekels were given for onion
bulbs for planting. Sheep in the reign of Cambyses
fetched 7 and 7¼ shekels each, while 10 shekels were
given for an ox, and 22½ shekels for a steer two years
old. In the twenty-fourth year of Nebuchadnezzar
13 shekels had been paid for a full-grown ox, and as
much as 67 shekels in the fourth year of Nabonidos,

while in the first year of Evil-Merodach a cow was
sold for 15 shekels. The ass was in more request,
especially if it was of " Western " breed. In the reign
of Merodach-nadin-akhi, it will be remembered, as
much as 130 shekels had been paid for one of these,
as compared with 30 shekels given for an ox, and
though at a subsequent period the prices were lower,
the animal was still valued highly. In the year of
the death of Cyrus a Babylonian gentleman bought
" a mouse-colored ass, eight years old, without blem-
ish," for 50 shekels (£7 10s.), and shortly afterward
another was purchased for 32 shekels. At the same
time, however, an ass of inferior quality went for
only 13 shekels. When we consider that only three
years later a shekel was considered sufficient wages
for a butcher for a month's work, we can better estimate what these prices signify. Nevertheless, the
value of the ass seems to have been steadily going
down in Babylonia; at all events, in the fourth year
of Nabonidos, 1 maneh, or 60 shekels, was demanded for one, and the animal does not seem to have
been in any way superior to another which was sold
for 50 shekels a few years afterward.

Clothes and woven stuffs were naturally of all
prices. In the time of Nebuchadnezzar a cloak or
overcoat used by the mountaineers cost only 4½
shekels, though under Cambyses we hear of 58 shekels
being charged for eight of the same articles of dress,
which were supplied to the " bowmen " of the army.
Three years earlier 7½ shekels had been paid for two
of these cloaks. About the same time ten sleeved
gowns cost 35 shekels.

Metal was more expensive. As has already been noticed, a copper libation-bowl and cup were sold for 4 manehs 9 shekels (£37 7s.), and two copper dishes, weighing 7½ manehs (19 pounds 8 ounces. troy), were valued at 22 shekels. The skilled labor expended upon the work was the least part of the cost. The workman was supplied with his materials by the customer, and received only the value of his labor. What this was can be gathered from a receipt dated the 11th day of Chisleu, in the fourteenth year of Nabonidos, recording the payment of 4 shekels to "the ironsmith," Suqâ, for making certain objects out of 3⅝ manehs of iron which had been handed over to him.

The cost of bricks and reeds has already been described. Bitumen was more valuable. In the fourteenth year of Nabonidos a contract was made to supply five hundred loads of it for 50 shekels, while at the same time the wooden handle of an ax was estimated at one shekel. Five years previously only 2 shekels had been given for three hundred wooden handles, but they were doubtless intended for knives. In the sixth year of Nabonidos the grandson of the priest of Sippara undertook to supply "bricks, reeds, beams, doors, and chopped straw for building the house of Rimut" for 12 manehs of silver, or £108. The wages of the workmen were not included in the contract.

With these prices it is instructive to compare those recorded on contract-tablets of the age of the third dynasty of Ur, which preceded that under which Abraham was born. These tablets, though very numerous, have as yet been but little examined, and the system of weights and measures which they contain is still but imperfectly known. We learn from them that bitumen could be purchased at the time at the rate of half a shekel of silver for each talent of 60 manehs, and that logs of wood imported from abroad were sold at the rate of eight, ten, twelve, and sixty logs a shekel, the price varying according to the nature of the wood. Prices, however, as might be expected, are usually calculated in grain, oil, and the like, and the exact relation of these to the shekel and maneh has still to be determined.

The average wages of the workmen can be more easily fixed. Contracts dated in the reign of Kham-murabi, the Amraphel of Genesis, and found at Sip-para, show that it was at the rate of about 4 shekels a year, the laborer's food being usually thrown in as well. Thus in one of these contracts we read: "Rimmon-bani has hired Sumi-izzitim for his brother, as a laborer, for three months, his wages to be one shekel and a half of silver, three measures of flour, and 1 qa and a half of oil. There shall be no withdrawal from the agreement. Ibni-amurru and Sikni-Anunit have endorsed it. Rimmon-bani has hired the laborer in the presence of Abum-ilu (Abimael), the son of Ibni-samas, of Ili-su-ibni, the son of Igas-Rimmon; and Arad-Bel, the son of Akhuwam." [1] Then follows the date. Another contract of the same age is of much the same tenor. "Nur-Rimmon has taken Idiyatum, the son of Ili-kamma, from Naram-bani, to work for him for a year at a yearly wage of 4½

[1] See above, p. 23 f.

shekels of silver. At the beginning of the month
Sebat, Idiyatum shall enter upon his service, and in
the month Iyyar it shall come to an end and he shall
quit it. Witnessed by Beltani, the daughter of Araz-
za; by Beltani, the daughter of Mudadum; by Amat-
Samas, the daughter of Asarid-ili; by Arad-izzitim,
the son of Samas-mutasi; and by Amat-Bau, the
priestess (?); the year when the Temple of the Abundance of Rimmon (was built by Khammurabi)." It
will be noticed that with one exception the witnesses
to this document are all women.

There was but little rise in wages in subsequent
centuries. A butcher was paid only 1 shekel for a
month's work in the third year of Cambyses, as has
been noticed above, and even skilled labor was not
much better remunerated. In the first year of Cambyses, for instance, only half a shekel was paid for
painting the stucco of a wall, though in the same
year 67 shekels (£10 1s.) were given to a seal-cutter
for a month's labor. Slavery prevented wages from
rising by flooding the labor market, and the free artisan had to compete with a vast body of slaves.
Hence it was that unskilled work was still so commonly paid in kind rather than in coin, and that the
workman was content if his employer provided him
with food. Thus in the second year of Nabonidos we
are told that the "coppersmith," Libludh, received
7 qas (about 8½ quarts) of flour for overlaying a
chariot with copper, and in the seventeenth year of
the same reign half a shekel of silver and 1 gur of
wheat from the royal storehouse were paid to five
men who had brought a flock of sheep to the King's

administrator in the city of Ruzabu.   The following
laconic letter also tells the same tale: " Letter from
Tabik-zeri to Gula-ibni, my brother.   Give 54 *qas* of
meal to the men who have dug the canal.   The 9th
of Nisan, fifth year of Cyrus, King of Eridu, King of
the World."   The employer had a right to the workman's labor so long as he furnished him with food
and clothing.

CHAPTER VII

THE MONEY-LENDER AND BANKER

AMONG the professions of ancient Babylonia, money-lending held a foremost place. It was, in fact, one of the most lucrative of professions, and was followed by all classes of the population, the highest as well the lowest. Members of the royal family did not disdain to lend money at high rates of interest, receiving as security for it various kinds of property. It is true that in such cases the business was managed by an agent; but the lender of the money, and not the agent, was legally responsible for all the consequences of his action, and it was to him that all the profits went.

The money-lender was the banker of antiquity. In a trading community like that of Babylonia, where actual coin was comparatively scarce, and the gigantic system of credit which prevails in the modern world had not as yet come into existence, it was impossible to do without him. The taxes had to be paid in cash, which was required by the government for the payment of a standing army, and a large body of officials. The same causes which have thrown the fellahin of modern Egypt into the hands of Greek usurers were at work in ancient Babylonia.

In some instances the money-lender founded a business which lasted for a number of generations and brought a large part of the property of the country into the possession of the firm. This was notably the case with the great firm of Egibi, established at Babylon before the time of Sennacherib, which in the age of the Babylonian empire and Persian conquest became the Rothschilds of the ancient world. It lent money to the state as well as to individuals, it undertook agencies for private persons, and eventually absorbed a good deal of what was properly attorney's business. Deeds and other legal documents belonging to others as well as to members of the firm were lodged for security in its record-chambers, stored in the great earthenware jars which served as safes. The larger part of the contract-tablets from which our knowledge of the social life of later Babylonia is derived has come from the offices of the firm.

In the early days of Babylonia the interest upon a loan was paid in kind.

But the introduction of a circulating medium goes back to an ancient date, and it was not long before payment in grain or other crops was replaced by its equivalent in cash. Already before the days of Amraphel and Abraham, we find contracts stipulating for the payment of so many silver shekels per month upon each maneh lent to the borrower. Thus we have one written in Semitic-Babylonian which reads: "Kisnunu, the son of Imur-Sin, has received one maneh and a half of silver from Zikilum, on which he will pay 12 shekels of silver (a month). The capital and interest are to be paid on the day of the harvest as guaranteed. Dated the year when Immerum dug the Asukhi canal." Then follow the names of three witnesses.

The obligation to repay the loan on "the day of the harvest" is a survival from the time when all payments were in kind, and the creditor had a right to the first-fruits of the debtor's property. A contract dated in the reign of Khammurabi, or Amraphel, similarly stipulates that interest on a loan made to a certain Arad-ilisu by one of the female devotees of the Sun-god, should be paid into the treasury of the temple of Samas "on the day of the harvest." The interest was reckoned at so much a month, as in the East to-day; originally it had to be paid at the end of each month, according to the literal terms of the agreement, but as time went on it became usual to reserve the payment to the end of six months or a year. It was only where the debtor was not considered trustworthy or the security was insufficient that the literal interpretation of the agreement was insisted on.

The rate of interest, as was natural, tended to be lower with the lapse of time and the growth of wealth. In the age of the Babylonian empire and the Persian conquest the normal rate was, however, still as high as 1 shekel a month upon each maneh, or twenty per cent. But we have a contract dated in the fifth year of Nebuchadnezzar in which a talent of silver is lent, and the interest charged upon it is not more than half a shekel per month on the maneh, or ten per cent. Three years later, in another contract, the rate of interest is stated to be five-sixths of a shekel, or sixteen and two-thirds per cent., while in the fifteenth year of Samas-sum-yukin the interest upon a loan of 16 shekels is only a quarter of a shekel. At this time Babylonia was suffering from the results of its revolt from Assyria, which may explain the lowness of the rate of interest. At all events, six years earlier, Remut, one of the members of the Egibi firm, lent a sum of money to a man and his wife without charging any interest at all upon it, and stipulating only that the money should be repaid when the land was again prosperous.

At times, however, money was lent upon the under-standing that interest would be charged upon it only if it were not repaid by a specified date. Thus in the ninth year of Samas-sum-yukin half a maneh was lent by Suma to Tukubenu on the fourth of Marches-van, or October, upon which no interest was to be paid up to the end of the following Tisri, or September, which corresponded with " the day of the harvest " of the older contracts ; but after that, if the money were still unpaid, interest at the rate of half a shekel a month, or ten per cent., would be charged. At other times the interest was paid by the year, as with us, and not by the month ; in this case it was at a lower rate than the normal twenty per cent. In the four-teenth year of Nabopolassar, for example, a maneh of silver was lent at the rate of 7 shekels on each maneh per annum—that is to say, at eleven and two-thirds per cent.—and under Nebuchadnezzar money was borrowed at annual interest of 8 shekels for each maneh, or thirteen and one-third per cent.

Full security was taken for a loan, and the contract relating to it was attested by a number of witnesses.

Thus the following contract was drawn up in the third year of Nabonidos, a loan of a maneh of silver having been made by one of the members of the Egibi firm to a man and his wife: "One maneh of silver, the property of Nadin-Merodach, the son of Iqisa-bel, the son of Nur-sin, has been received by Nebo-baladan, the son of Nadin-sumi, and Bau-ed-herat, the daughter of Samas-ebus. In the month Tisri (September) they shall repay the money and the interest upon it. Their upper field, which adjoins that of Sum-yukin, the son of Sa-Nebo-sû, as well as the lower field, which forms the boundary of the house of the Seer, and is planted with palm-trees and grass, is the security of Nadin-Merodach, to which (in case of insolvency) he shall have the first claim. No other creditor shall take possession of it until Nadin-Merodach has received in full the capital and interest. In the month Tisri the dates which are then ripe upon the palms shall be valued, and according to the current price of them at the time in the town of Sakhrin, Nadin-Merodach shall accept them instead of interest at the rate of thirty-six *qas* (fifty quarts) the shekel (3s.). The money is intended to pay the tax for providing the soldiers of the king of Babylon with arms. Witnessed by Nebo-bel-sunu, the son of Bau-akhi, the son of Dahik; Nebo-dîni-ebus, the son of Kinenunâ; Nebo-zira-usabsi, the son, Samas-ibni Bazuzu, the son of Samas-ibni; Mero-dach-erba, the son of Nadin; and the scribe Bel-iddin, the son of Bel-yupakhkhir, the son of Dabibu. Dated at Sakhrinni, the 28th day of Iyyar (April), the third year of Nabonidos, King of Babylon."

In Assyria the rate of interest was a good deal higher than it was in Babylonia. It is true that in a contract dated 667 B.C., one of the parties to which was
the son of the secretary of the municipality of Dur-
Sargon, the modern Khorsabad, it is twenty per cent.,
as in Babylonia, but this is almost the only case in
which it is so.   Elsewhere, in deeds dated 684 B.C.,
656, and later, the rate is as much as twenty-five per
cent., while in one instance—a deed dated 711 B.C.—
it rises to thirty-three and a third per cent. Among
the witnesses to the last-mentioned deed are two
" smiths," one of whom is described as a "coppersmith," and the other bears the Armenian name of
Sihduri or Sarduris.   The money is usually reckoned
according to the standard of Carchemish.   That the
rate of interest should have been higher in Assyria
than in Babylonia is not surprising.   Commerce was
less developed there, and the attention of the population was devoted rather to war and agriculture than
to trade.   It seems to have been the conquest of
Western Asia, the subjugation of the Phœnician cities,
and above all the incorporation of Babylonia in the
empire, which introduced a commercial spirit into
Nineveh, and made it in the latter days of its existence an important centre of trade.   Indeed, one of
the objects of the Assyrian campaigns in Syria was
to divert the trade of the Mediterranean into Assyrian hands ; the fall of Carchemish made Assyria
mistress of the caravan-road which led across the
Euphrates, and of the commerce which had flowed
from Asia Minor, while the ruin of Tyre and Sidon
meant prosperity to the merchants of Nineveh.   Nev-

ertheless, the native population of Assyria was slow
to avail itself of the commercial advantages which
had fallen to it, and a large part of its trading classes
were Arameans or other foreigners who had settled
in the country. So large, indeed, was the share in
Assyrian trade which the Arameans absorbed that
Aramaic became the *lingua panca*, the common medium of intercommunication, in the commercial world
of the second Assyrian empire, and, as has been already stated, many of the Assyrian contract-tablets
are provided with Aramaic dockets, which give a
brief abstract of their contents.

A memorandum signed by "Basia, the son of
Rikhi," furnishes us with the relative value of gold
and silver in the age of Nebuchadnezzar. "Two
shekels and a quarter of gold for twenty-five shekels
and three-quarters of silver, one shekel worn and defi-
cient in weight for seven shekels of silver, two and a
quarter shekels, also worn, for twenty-two and three-
quarters shekels of silver; in all five and a half shekels
of gold for fifty-five and a half shekels of silver."
Gold, therefore, at this time would have been worth
about eleven times more than silver. A few years
later, however, in the eleventh year of Nabonidos, the
proportion had risen and was twelve to one. We
learn this from a statement that the goldsmith Nebo-
edhernapisti had received in that year, on the 10th
day of Ab, 1 shekel of gold, in 5-shekel pieces, for 12
shekels of silver. The coinage, if we may use such
a term, was the same in both metals, the talent being divided into 60 manehs and the maneh into 60
shekels. There seems also to have been a bronze

coinage, at all events in the later age of Assyria and Babylonia, but the references to it are very scanty, and silver was the ordinary medium of exchange. One of the contract-tablets, however, which have come from Assyria and is dated in the year 676 B.C., relates to the loan of 2 talents of bronze from the treasury of Istar at Arbela, which were to be repaid two months afterward. Failing this, interest was to be charged upon them at the rate of thirty-three and a third per cent., and it is implied that the payment was to be in bronze.

The talent, maneh, and shekel were originally weights, and had been adopted by the Semites from their Sumerian predecessors. They form part of that sexagesimal system of numeration which lay at the root of Babylonian mathematics and was as old as the invention of writing. So thoroughly was sixty regarded as the unit of calculation that it was denoted by the same single wedge or upright line as that which stood for "one." Wherever the sexagesimal system of notation prevailed we may see an evidence of the influence of Babylonian culture.

It was the maneh, however, and not the talent, which was adopted as the standard. The talent, in fact, was too heavy for such a purpose; it implied too considerable an amount of precious metal and was too seldom employed in the daily business of life. The Babylonian, accordingly, counted up from the maneh to the talent and down to the shekel.

The standard weight of the maneh, which continued in use up to the latest days of Babylonian history, had been fixed by Dungi, of the dynasty of Ur,

about 2700 B.C. An inscription on a large cone of
dark-green stone, now in the British Museum, tells
us that the cone represents "one maneh standard
weight, the property of Merodach-sar-ilani, and a
duplicate of the weight which Nebuchadnezzar, king
of Babylon, the son of Nabopolassar, king of Babylon, had made in exact imitation of the standard
weight established by the deified Dungi, an earlier
king." The stone now weighs 978.309 grammes,
which, making the requisite deductions for the wear
and tear of time, would give 980 grammes, or rather
more than 2 pounds 2 ounces avoirdupois. The
Babylonian maneh, as fixed by Dungi and Nebuchadnezzar, thus agrees in weight rather with the Hebrew
maneh of gold than with the "royal" maneh, which
was equivalent to 2 pounds 7½ ounces.

It was not, however, the only maneh in use in
Babylonia. Besides the "heavy" or "royal" maneh
there was also a "light" maneh, like the Hebrew
silver maneh of 1 pound 11 ounces, while the Assyrian contract-tablets make mention of "the maneh
of Carchemish," which was introduced into Assyria
after the conquest of the Hittite capital in 717 B.C.
Mr. Barclay V. Head has pointed out that this latter
maneh was known in Asia Minor as far as the shores
of the Ægean, and that the "tongues" or bars of silver found by Dr. Schliemann on the site of Troy
are shekels made in accordance with it.[1]

---

[1] Schliemann, Ilios, pp. 471, 472. Mr. Head shows that the
maneh in question is identical with the Babylonian silver maneh of
8,656 grains troy, or 561 grammes, though the latter is now more
usually fixed at 546 grammes.

A similar "tongue" of gold "of fifty shekels weight" is referred to in Josh. vii. 21, in connection with that "goodly Babylonish garment" which was carried away by Achan from among the spoils of Jericho. It is probable that the shekels and manehs of Babylonia were originally cast in the same tongue-like form. In Egypt they were in the shape of rings and spirals, but there is no evidence that the use of the latter extended beyond the valley of the Nile. In Western Asia it was rather bars of metal that were employed.

At first the value of the bar had to be determined by its being weighed each time that it changed hands. But it soon came to be stamped with an official indication of its weight and value. A Cappadocian tablet found near Kaisariyeh, which is at least as early as the age of the Exodus and may go back to that of Abraham, speaks of "three shekels of sealed" or "stamped silver." In that distant colony of Babylonian civilization, therefore, an official seal was already put upon some of the money in circulation. In the time of Nebuchadnezzar the coinage was still more advanced. There were "single shekel" pieces, pieces of "five shekels" and the like, all implying that coins were issued representing different fractions of the maneh. The maneh itself was divided into pieces of five-sixths, two-thirds, one-third, one-half, one-quarter, and three-quarters. It is often specified whether a sum of money is to be paid in single shekel pieces or in 5-shekel pieces, and the word "stamped" is sometimes added. The invention of a regular coinage is generally ascribed to the

Lydians ; but it was more probably due to the Baby-lonians, from whom both Lydians and Greeks derived their system of weights as well as the term *mina* or maneh.

The Egibi firm was not the only great banking or trading establishment of which we know in ancient Babylonia. The American excavators at Niffer have brought to light the records of another firm, that of Murasu, which, although established in a provincial town and not in the capital, rose to a position of great wealth and influence under the Persian kings Artaxerxes I. (464–424 B.C.) and Darius II. (424–405 B.C.). The tablets found at Tello also indicate the existence of similarly important trading firms in the Babylonia of 2700 B.C., though at this period trade was chiefly confined to home products, cattle and sheep, wool and grain, dates and bitumen.

The learned professions were well represented. The scribes were a large and powerful body, and in Assyria, where education was less widely diffused than in Babylonia, they formed a considerable part of the governing bureaucracy. In Babylonia they acted as librarians, authors, and publishers, multi-plying copies of older books and adding to them new works of their own. They served also as clerks and secretaries ; they drew up documents of state as well as legal contracts and deeds. They were accordingly responsible for the forms of legal procedure, and so to some extent occupied the place of the barristers and attorneys of to-day. The Baby-lonian seems usually, if not always, to have pleaded his own case ; but his statement of it was thrown

into shape by the scribe or clerk like the final decision of the judges themselves. Under Nebuchadnezzar and his successors such clerks were called " the
scribes of the king," and were probably paid out of
the public revenues. Thus in the second year of Evil-
Merodach it is said of the claimants to an inheritance
that " they shall speak to the scribes of the king and
seal the deed," and the seller of some land has to
take the deed of quittance "to the scribes of the
king," who "shall supervise and seal it in the city."
Many of the scribes were priests; and it is not uncommon to find the clerk who draws up a contract
and appears as a witness to be described as "the
priest " of some deity.

The physician is mentioned at a very early date.
Thus we hear of " Ilu-bani, the physician of Gudea,"
the High-priest of Lagas (2700 B.C.), and a treatise
on medicine, of which fragments exist in the British
Museum, was compiled long before the days of Abraham. It continued to be regarded as a standaad
work on the subject even in the time of the second
Assyrian empire, though its prescriptions are mixed
up with charms and incantations. But an attempt
was made in it to classify and describe various diseases, and to enumerate the remedies that had been
proposed for them. The remedies are often a compound of the most heterogeneous drugs, some of
which are of a very unsavory nature. However, the
patient, or his doctor, is generally given a choice of
the remedies he might adopt. Thus for an attack of
spleen he was told either to " slice the seed of a reed
and dates in palm-wine," or to " mix calves' milk and

bitters in palm-wine," or to "drink garlic and bitters in palm-wine." "For an aching tooth," it is laid down, "the plant of human destiny (perhaps the mandrake) is the remedy; it must be placed upon the tooth. The fruit of the yellow snakewort is another remedy for an aching tooth; it must be placed upon the tooth. . . . The roots of a thorn which does not see the sun when growing is another remedy for an aching tooth; it must be placed upon the tooth." Unfortunately it is still impossible to assign a precise signification to most of the drugs that are named, or to identify the various herbs contained in the Babylonian pharmacopœia.

As time passed on, the charms and other superstitious practices which had at first played so large a part in Babylonian medicine fell into the background and were abandoned to the more uneducated classes of society. The conquest of Western Asia by the Egyptian Pharaohs of the eighteenth dynasty brought Babylonia into contact with Egypt, where the art of medicine was already far advanced. It is probable that from this time forward Babylonian medicine also became more strictly scientific. We have indeed evidence that the medical system and practice of Egypt had been introduced into Asia. When the great Egyptian treatise on medicine, known as the Papyrus Ebers, was written in the sixteenth century B.C., one of the most fashionable oculists of the day was a "Syrian" of Gebal, and as the study of the disease of the eye was peculiarly Egyptian, we must assume that his science had been derived from the valley of the Nile. It must not be supposed, however, that

the superstitious beliefs and practices of the past
were altogether abandoned, even by the most distinguished practitioners, any more than they were by
the physicians of Europe in the early part of the last
century. But they were invoked only when the ordinary remedies had failed, and when no resource
seemed left except the aid of spiritual powers.
Otherwise the doctor depended upon his diagnosis
of the disease and the prescriptions which had been
accumulated by the experience of past generations.

At the head of the profession stood the court-
physician, the Rab-mugi or Rab-mag as he was
called in Babylonia. In Assyria there was more
than one doctor attached to the royal person, but letters have come down to us from which we learn that
the royal physicians were at times permitted to attend private individuals when they were sick. Thus
we have a letter of thanks to the Assyrian King from
one of his subjects full of gratitude to the King for
sending his own doctor to the writer, who had accordingly been cured of a dangerous disease. " May
Istar of Erech," he says, " and Nana (of Bit-Anu)
grant long life to the king my lord, for he has sent
Basa, the royal physician, to save my life, and he has
cured me ; may the great gods of heaven and earth
be therefore gracious to the king my lord, and may
they establish the throne of the king my lord in
heaven for ever, since I was dead and the king has
restored me to life." Another letter contains a petition that one of the royal physicians should be allowed to visit a lady who was ill. " To the king my
lord," we read, "thy servant, Saul-miti-yuballidh,

sends salutation to the king my lord : may Nebo and
Merodach be gracious to the king my lord for ever
and ever. Bau-gamilat, the handmaid of the king, is
constantly ill; she cannot eat a morsel of food. Let
the king send orders that some physician may go and
see her." In this case, however, it is possible that
the lady, who seems to have been suffering from con-
sumption, belonged to the harîm of the monarch, and
it was consequently needful to obtain the royal permission for a stranger to visit her, even though he
came professionally.

We can hardly reckon among Babylonian professions that of the poet. It is true that a sort of poet-
laureate existed at the court, and that we hear of a
piece of land being given by the King to one of them
for some verses which he had composed in honor of
the sovereign. But poetry was not a separate profession, and the poet must be included in the class
of scribes, or among those educated country gentlemen who possessed estates of their own. He was,
however, fully appreciated in Babylonia. The names
of the chief poets of the country were never forgotten,
and the poems they had written passed through edition after edition down to the later days of Babylonian history. Sin-liqi-unnini, the author of the "Epic
of Gilgames," Nis-Sin, the author of the "Adventures
of Etana," and many others, never passed out of literary remembrance. There was a large reading public, and the literary language of Babylonia changed
but little from century to century.

It was otherwise with the musicians. They formed
a class to themselves, though whether as a trade or

as a profession it is difficult to say. We must, however, distinguish between the composer and the performer. The latter was frequently a slave or captive, and occupied but an humble place in society. He is frequently depicted in the Assyrian bas-reliefs, and in one instance is represented as wearing a cap of great height and shaped like a fish. Musical instruments were numerous and various. We find among them drums and tambourines, trumpets and horns, lyres and guitars, harps and zithers, pipes and cymbals. Even the speaking-trumpet was employed. In a sculpture which represents the transport of a colossal bull from the quarries of Balad to the palace of Sennacherib, an overseer is made to stand on the body of the bull and issue orders through a trumpet to the workmen.

Besides single musicians, there were bands of performers, and at times the music was accompanied by dancing or by clapping the hands. The bands were under the conduct of leaders, who kept time with a double rod. In one instance the Assyrian artist has represented three captives playing on a lyre, an interesting illustration of the complaint of the Jewish exiles in Babylonia that their conquerors required from them "a song."

The artist fared no better than the musical performer. The painter of the figures and scenes on the walls of the chamber, the sculptor of the bas-reliefs which adorned an Assyrian palace, or of the statues which stood in the temples of Babylonia, the engraver of the gems and seals, some of which show such high artistic talent, were all alike skilled artisans and nothing more.

We have already seen what wages they received, and
what consequently must have been the social admira-
tion in which they were held.   Behind the workman,
however, stood the original artist, who conceived and
drew the first designs, and to whom the artistic inspiration was primarily due.   Of him we still know
nothing.   Probably he belonged in general to the
class of priests or scribes, and would have disdained
to receive remuneration for his art.   As yet the texts
have thrown no light upon him, and it may be that
they never will do so.   The Babylonians were a practical and not an artistic people, and the skilled artisan gave them all that they demanded in the matter
of art.

CHAPTER VIII

THE GOVERNMENT AND THE ARMY

THE conception of the state in Babylonia was intensely theocratic. The kings had been preceded by high-priests, and up to the last they performed priestly functions, and represented the religious as well as the civil power. At Babylon the real sovereign was Bel Merodach, the true "lord" of the city, and it was only when the King had been adopted by the god as his son that he possessed any right to rule. Before he had "taken the hands" of Bel, and thereby become the adopted son of the deity, he had no legitimate title to the throne. He was, in fact, the vicegerent and representative of Bel upon earth; it was Bel who gave him his authority and watched over him as a father over a son.

The Babylonian sovereign was thus quite as much a pontiff as he was a king. The fact was acknowledged in the titles he bore, as well as in the ceremony which legitimized his accession to the throne. Two views prevailed, however, as to his relation to the god. According to one of these, sonship conferred upon him actual divinity; he was not merely the representative of a god, but a god himself. This was the view which prevailed in the earlier days of Semitic supremacy.

Sargon of Akkad and his son Naram-Sin are entitled
"gods ; " temples and priests were dedicated to them
during their lifetime, and festivals were observed in
their honor. Their successors claimed and received
the same attributes of divinity. Under the third
dynasty of Ur even the local prince, Gudea, the high-
priest of Tello, was similarly deified. It was not
until Babylonia had been conquered by the foreign
Kassite dynasty from the mountains of Elam that a
new conception of the King was introduced. He
ceased to be a god himself, and became, instead, the
delegate and representative of the god of whom he
was the adopted son. His relation to the god was
that of a son during the lifetime of his father, who
can act for his father, but cannot actually take the
father's place so long as the latter is alive.

Some of the earlier Chaldean monarchs call themselves sons of the goddesses who were worshipped in
the cities over which they held sway. They thus
claimed to be of divine descent, not by adoption, but
by actual birth. The divinity that was in them was
inherited ; it was not merely communicated by a later
and artificial process. The "divine right," by grace
of which they ruled, was the right of divine birth.

At the outset, therefore, the Babylonian King was
a pontiff because he was also a god. In him the
deities of heaven were incarnated on earth. He
shared their essence and their secrets ; he knew how
their favor could be gained or their enmity averted,
and so mediated between god and man. This deification of the King, however, cannot be traced beyond the
period when Semitic rule was firmly established in

Chaldea. It is true that Sumerian princes, like Gudea of Lagas, were also deified; but this was long after the rise of Semitic supremacy, and the age of Sargon of Akkad, and when Sumerian culture was deeply interpenetrated by Semitic ideas. So far as we know at present the apotheosis of the King was of Semitic origin.

It is paralleled by the apotheosis of the King in ancient Egypt. There, too, the Pharaoh was regarded as an incarnation of divinity, to whom shrines were erected, priests ordained, and sacrifices offered. In early times he was, moreover, declared to be the son of the goddess of the city in which he dwelt; it was not till the rise of the fifth historical dynasty that he became the "Son of the Sun-god" of Heliopolis, rather than Horus, the Sun-god, himself. This curious parallelism is one of many facts which point to intercourse between Babylonia and Egypt in the prehistoric age; whether the deification of the King originated first on the banks of the Euphrates or of the Nile must be left to the future to decide.

Naram-Sin is addressed as "the god of Agadê," or Akkad, the capital of his dynasty, and long lists have been found of the offerings that were made, month by month, to the deified Dungi, King of Ur, and his vassal, Gudea of Lagas. Here, for example, are Dr. Scheil's translations of some of them: "I. Half a measure of good beer and 5 *gin* of sesame oil on the new moon, the 15th day, for the god Dungi; half a measure of good beer and half a measure of herbs for Gudea the High-priest, during the month Tammuz. II. Half a measure of the king's good beer, half a measure of herbs, on the new moon, the 15th day, for Gudea the High-priest. One measure of good wort beer, 5 *qas* of ground flour, 3 *qas* of cones (?), for the planet Mercury: during the month of the festival of the god Dungi. III. . . . Half a measure of good beer, half a measure of herbs, on the new moon, the 15th day, for the god Gudea the High-priest: during the month Elul, the first year of Gimil-Sin, king [of Ur]."

The conception of the King as a visible god upon earth was unable to survive the conquest of Babylonia by the half-civilized mountaineers of Elam and the substitution of foreigners for the Semitic or Semitized Sumerian rulers of the country. As the doctrine of the divine right of kings passed away in England with the rise of the Hanoverian dynasty, so, too, in Babylonia the deified King disappeared with the Kassite conquest. But he continued to be supreme pontiff to the adopted son of the god of Babylon. Babylon had become the capital of the kingdom, and Merodach, its patron-deity, was, accordingly, supreme over the other gods of Chaldea. He alone could confer the royal powers that the god of every city which was the centre of a principality had once been qualified to grant. By "taking his hands" the King became his adopted son, and so received a legitimate right to the throne.

It was the throne not only of Babylonia, but of the Babylonian empire as well. It was never forgotten that Babylonia had once been the mistress of Western Asia, and it was, accordingly, the sceptre of Western Asia that was conferred by Bel-Merodach upon his

adopted sons. Like the Holy Roman Empire in the
Middle Ages, Babylonian sovereignty brought with it
a legal, though shadowy, right to rule over the civilized kingdoms of the world. It was this which made
the Assyrian conquerors of the second Assyrian empire so anxious to secure possession of Babylon and
there "take the hands of Bel." Tiglath-pileser III.,
Shalmaneser IV., and Sargon were all alike usurpers,
who governed by right of the sword. It was only
when they had made themselves masters of Babylon
and been recognized by Bel and his priesthood that
their title to govern became legitimate and unchal-
lenged.

Cyrus and Cambyses continued the tradition of the
native kings. They, too, claimed to be the successors
of those who had ruled over Western Asia, and Bel,
of his own free choice, it was alleged, had rejected the
unworthy Nabonidos and put Cyrus in his place.
Cyrus ruled, not by right of conquest, but because he
had been called to the crown by the god of Babylon.
It was not until the Zoroastrean Darius and Xerxes
had taken Babylon by storm and destroyed the temple of Bel that the old tradition was finally thrust
aside. The new rulers of Persia had no belief in the
god of Babylon; his priesthood was hostile to them,
and Babylon was deposed from the position it had so
long occupied as the capital of the world.

In Assyria, in contrast to Babylonia, the government rested on a military basis. It is true that
the kings of Assyria had once been the high-priests
of the city of Assur, and that they carried with
them some part of their priestly functions when

they were invested with royal power. But it is
no less true that they were never looked upon as
incarnations of the deity or even as his representative upon earth. The rise of the Assyrian kingdom seems to have been due to a military revolt;
at any rate, its history is that of a succession of
rebellious generals, some of whom succeeded in
founding dynasties, while others failed to hand down
their power to their posterity. There was no religious ceremony at their coronation like that of "taking the hands of Bel." When Esar-haddon was
made King he was simply acclaimed sovereign by the
army. It was the army and not the priesthood to
whom he owed his title to reign.

The conception of the supreme god himself differed in Assyria and Babylonia. In Babylonia, Bel-
Merodach was "lord" of the city; in Assyria, Assur
was the deified city itself. In the one case, therefore, the King was appointed vicegerent of the god
over the city which he governed and preserved; in
the other case the god represented the state, and, in
so far as the King was a servant of the god, he was a
servant also of the state.

In both countries there was an aristocracy of birth
based originally on the possession of land. But in
Babylonia it tended at an early period to be absorbed by the mercantile and priestly classes, and
in later days it is difficult to find traces even of its
existence. The nobles of the age of Nebuchadnezzar
were either wealthy trading families or officers of the
Crown. The temples, and the priests who lived upon
their revenues, had swallowed up a considerable part

of the landed and other property of the country,
which had thus become what in modern Turkey would
be called *wakf.* In Assyria many of the great princes
of the realm still belonged to the old feudal aristocracy, but here again the tendency was to replace
them by a bureaucracy which owed its position and
authority to the direct favor of the King.   Under
Tiglath-pileser III. this tendency became part of
the policy of the government; the older aristocracy
disappeared, and instead of it we find military officers and civil officials, all of whom were appointed by
the Crown.

While, accordingly, Babylonia became an industrial
and priestly state, Assyria developed into a great
military and bureaucratic organization.   It taught
the world how to organize and administer an empire.
Tiglath-pileser III. inaugurated a course of policy
which his successors did their best to carry out.   He
aimed at reviving the ancient empire of Sargon of
Akkad, of uniting the civilized world of Western
Asia under one head, but upon new principles and
in a more permanent way.   The campaigns which
his predecessors had carried on for the sake of booty
and military fame were now conducted with a set.
purpose and method.   The raid was replaced by a
carefully planned scheme of conquest.   The vanquished territories were organized into provinces
under governors appointed by the Assyrian King and
responsible to him alone.   By the side of the civil
governor was a military commander, who kept watch
upon the other's actions, while under them was a
large army of administrators.   Assyrian colonies

were planted in the newly acquired districts, where they served as a garrison, and the native inhabitants were transported to other parts of the Assyrian empire. In this way an attempt was made to break the old ties of patriotism and local feeling, and to substitute for them fidelity to the Assyrian government and the god Assur, in whose name its conquests were made.

The taxes of the empire were carefully regulated. A cadastral survey was an institution which had long been in existence; it had been borrowed from Babylonia, where, as we have seen, it was already known at a very early epoch. The amount to be paid into the treasury by each town and province was fixed, and the governor was called upon to transmit it each year to Nineveh. Thus in the time of Sennacherib the annual tribute of Carchemish was 100 talents, that of Arpad 30, and that of Megiddo 15, while, at home, Nineveh was assessed at 30 talents, and the district of Assur at 20, which were expended on the maintenance of the fleet, the whole amount of revenue raised from Assyria being 274 talents. Besides this direct taxation, there was also indirect taxation, as well as municipal rates. Thus a tax was laid upon the brick-fields, which in Babylonia were economically of considerable importance, and there was an *octroi* duty upon all goods, cattle, and country produce which entered a town. Similar tolls were exacted from the ships which moored at the quays, as well as from those who made use of the pontoon-bridges which spanned the Euphrates or passed under them in boats.

Long lists of officials have been preserved. Certain of the governors or satraps were allowed to share with the King the privilege of giving a name to the year. It was an ingenious system of reckoning time which had been in use in Assyria from an early period and was introduced into Cappadocia by Assyrian colonists. From Asia Minor it probably spread to Greece ; at all events, the eponymous archons at Athens, after whom the several years were named, corresponded exactly with the Assyrian *limmi* or eponyms. Each year in succession received its name from the eponym or officer who held office during the course of it, and as lists of these officers were carefully handed down it was easy to determine the date of an event which had taken place in the year of office of a given eponym. The system was of Assyrian invention and never prevailed in Babylonia. There time was dated by the chief occurrences of a king's reign, and at the end of the reign a list of them was drawn up beginning with his accession to the throne and ending with his death and the name of his successor. These lists went back to an early period of Babylonian history and provided the future historian with an accurate chronology.

Immediately attached to the person of the Assyrian monarch was the Rab-saki, "the chief of the princes," or vizier. He is called the Rab-shakeh in the Old Testament, by the side of whom stood the Rab-saris, the Assyrian Rab-sa-risi, or "chief of the heads " of departments. They were both civil officers. The army was under the command of the Tartannu, or " Commander-in-Chief," the Biblical Tartan, who, in

the absence of the King, led the troops to battle
and conducted a campaign. When Shalmaneser II.,
for example, became too old to take the field himself,
his armies were led by the Tartan Daian-Assur, and
under the second Assyrian empire the Tartan appears frequently, sometimes in command of a portion
of the forces, while the King is employing the rest
elsewhere, sometimes in place of the King, who pre-
fers to remain at home. In earlier days there had
been two Tartans, one of whom stood on the right
hand side of the King and the other on his left. In
order of precedence both of them were regarded as
of higher rank than the Rab-shakeh.

The army was divided into companies of a thousand,
a hundred, fifty, and ten, and we hear of captains of
fifty and captains of ten. Under Tiglath-pileser III.
and his successors it became an irresistible engine
of attack. No pains were spared to make it as effective as possible; its discipline was raised to the highest pitch of perfection, and its arms and accoutrements constantly underwent improvements. As long
as a supply of men lasted, no enemy could stand
against it, and the great military empire of Nineveh
was safe.

It contained cavalry as well as foot-soldiers. The
cavalry had grown out of a corps of chariot-drivers,
which was retained, though shrunken in size and importance, long after the more serviceable horsemen
had taken its place. The chariot held a driver and a
warrior. When the latter was the King he was accompanied by one or two armed attendants. They
all rode standing and carried bows and spears. The

chariot itself ran upon two wheels, a pair of horses being harnessed to its pole. Another horse was often attached to it in case of accidents.

The chariots were of little good when the fighting had to be done in a mountainous country. In the level parts of Western Asia, where good roads had existed for untold centuries, they were a powerful arm of offence, but the Assyrians were constantly called upon to attack the tribes of the Kurdish and Armenian mountains who harassed their positions, and in such trackless districts the chariots were an incumbrance and not a help. Trees had to be cut down and rocks removed in order to make roads along which they might pass. The Assyrian engineers indeed were skilled in the construction of roads of the kind, and the inscriptions not infrequently boast of their success in carrying them through the most inaccessible regions, but the necessity for making them suitable for the passage of chariots was a serious drawback, and we hear at times how the wheels of the cars had to be taken off and the chariots conveyed on the backs of mules or horses. It was not wonderful, therefore, that the Assyrian kings, who were practical military men, soon saw the advantage of imitating the custom of the northern and eastern mountaineers, who used the horse for riding purposes rather than for drawing a chariot. The chariot continued to be employed in the Assyrian army, but rather as a luxury than as an effective instrument of war.

At first the cavalry were little more than mounted horsemen. Their only weapons were the bow and arrow, and they rode without saddles and with bare

legs.   At a later period part of the cavalry was armed
with spears, saddles were introduced, and the groom
who had run by the side of the horse disappeared.
At the same time, under Tiglath-pileser III., the
rider's legs were protected by leathern drawers over
which high boots were drawn, laced in front.   This
was an importation from the north, and it is possible
that many of the horsemen were brought from the
same quarter.   Sennacherib still further improved
the dress by adding to it a closely fitting coat of
mail.

The infantry outnumbered the cavalry by about ten
to one, and were divided into heavy-armed and light-
armed.   Their usual dress, at all events, up to the
foundation of the second Assyrian empire, consisted
of a peaked helmet and a tunic which descended half-
way down the thighs, and was fastened round the
waist by a girdle.   From the reign of Sargon onward
they were divided into two bodies, one of archers, the
other of spearmen, the archers being partly light-
armed and partly heavy-armed.   The heavy-armed
were again divided into two classes, one of them wearing sandals and a coat-of-mail over the tunic, while
the other was dressed in a long, fringed robe reaching
to the feet, over which a cuirass was worn.   They
also carried a short sword, and had sandals of the
same shape as those used by the other class.   Each
had an attendant waiting upon him with a long, rectangular shield of wicker-work, covered with leather.
The light-armed archers were encumbered with but
little clothing, consisting only of a kilt and a fillet
round the head.   The spearmen, on the contrary,

were protected by a crested helmet and circular shield, though their legs and face were usually bare.

Changes were introduced by Sennacherib, who abolished the inconveniently long robe of the second class of heavy-armed archers, and gave them leather greaves and boots. The first class, on the other hand, are now generally represented without sandals, and with an embroidered turban with lappets on the head. Sennacherib also established a corps of slingers, who were clad in helmet and breastplate, leather drawers, and short boots, as well as a company of pioneers, armed with double-headed axes, and clothed with conical helmets, greaves, and boots. These pioneers were especially needed for engineering the way through the pathless defiles and rugged ground over which the extension of the empire more and more required the Assyrian army to make its way.

The heads of the spears and arrows were of metal, usually of bronze, more rarely of iron. The helmets also were of bronze or iron, a leather cap being worn underneath them, and the coats-of-mail were formed of bronze scales sewn to a leather shirt. Many of the shields, moreover, were of metal, though wicker-work covered with leather seems to have been preferred. Battering-rams and other engines for attacking a city were carried on the march.

Baggage wagons were also carried, as well as standards and tents. The tents of the officers were divided into two partitions, one of which was used as a dining-room, while the royal tent was accompanied by a kitchen. Tables, chairs, couches, and various utensils formed part of its furniture. One of these chairs was a sort of palanquin in the shape of an arm-chair with a footstool, which was borne on the shoulders of attendants.

The Assyrian army was originally recruited from the native peasantry, who returned to their fields at the end of a campaign with the spoil that had been taken from the enemy. Under the second Assyrian empire, however, it became a standing army, a part of which was composed of mercenaries, while another part consisted of troops drafted from the conquered populations. Certain of the soldiers were selected to serve as the body-guard of the King; they had a commander of their own and doubtless possessed special privileges. The army was recruited by conscription, the obligation to serve in it being part of the burdens which had to be borne by the peasantry. They could be relieved of it by the special favor of the government just as they could be relieved of the necessity of paying taxes.

The Babylonian army of Nebuchadnezzar and his successors was modelled on that of the Assyrians. We can gather from the receipts for the provisions and accoutrements furnished to it how the army of Tiglath-pileser or Sennacherib must have been fed and paid. Thus in the first year of Nabonidos, 75 *qas* of flour and 63 *qas* (nearly 100 quarts) of beer were provided for the troops in the camp near Sippara, and in the second year of the same King 54 *qas* of beer were sent on the 29th of Nisan for "the soldiers who had marched from Babylon." Similarly in the tenth year of the same reign we have a receipt for the despatch of 116 *qas* of food on the

14th of Iyyar for "the troops which had marched
[to Sippara] from Babylon," as well as for 18 *qas*
of "provisions" provided each day for the same
purpose from the 15th to the 18th of the same
month. In the first year of Nabonidos 3 *gur* of
sesame had been ordered for the archers during
the first two months of the year, and as in his
thirteenth year 5 *gur* of wheat were provided for
fifteen soldiers, we may calculate that rather more
than two and one-half bushels were allotted to each
man. It may be added that at the beginning of
Nebuchadnezzar's reign we find a contractor guaranteeing "the excellence of the beer" that had been
furnished for the "army that had entered Babylon,"
though it is possible that here artisans rather than
soldiers are meant.

A register of the soldiers was kept, but it would
seem that those who were in charge of. it sometimes
forgot to strike off the names of those who were
dead or discharged, and pocketed their pay. At any
rate, the following official document has come down
to us :—"(The names) of the deserters and dead
soldiers which have been overlooked in the paymaster's account, the 8th day of Nisan, the eighth year
of Cyrus, king of Babylon and of the world : Samas-
akhi-iddin, son of Samas-ana-bitisu, deserted ; Muse-
zib-Samas, son of the Usian, *ditto ;* Itti-Samas-eneya
junior, of the family of Samas-kin-abli, *ditto ;* Itti-
Samas-baladhu, son of Samas-erba *ditto ;* Taddannu,
son of Rimut, *ditto ;* Samas-yuballidh, his brother,
ditto ; Kalbâ, son of Samas-kin-abli, son of the painter (?), *ditto ;* in all seven deserters.   Libludh, son of

Samas-edher, dead; Nebo-tuktê-tirri, *ditto;* Samas-mupakhkhiranni, *ditto;* Samas-akhi-erba, son of Sa-mas-ana-bitisu, *ditto;* in all four dead. Altogether eleven soldiers who have deserted or are dead."

If Babylonia copied Assyria in military arrangements, the converse was the case as regards a fleet. "The cry of the Chaldeans," according to the Old Testament, was "in their ships," and in the earliest age of Babylonian history, Eridu, which then stood on the sea-coast, was already a sea-port. But Assyria was too far distant from the sea for its inhabitants to become sailors, and the rapid current of the Tigris made even river navigation difficult. In fact, the rafts on which the heavy monuments were transported, and which could float only down stream, or the small, round boats, resembling the *kufas* that are still in use, were almost the only means employed for crossing the water. When the Assyrian army had to pass a river, either pontoons were thrown across it, or the soldiers swam across the streams with the help of inflated skins. The *kufa* was made of rushes daubed with bitumen, and sometimes covered with a skin.

So little accustomed were the Assyrians to navigation that, when Sennacherib determined to pursue the followers of Merodach-baladan across the Persian Gulf to the coast of Elam, he was obliged to have recourse to the Phœnician boat-builders and sailors. Two fleets were built for him by Phœnician and Syrian workmen, one at Tel-Barsip, near Carchemish, on the Euphrates, the other at Nineveh on the Tigris; these he manned with Syrian, Sidonian, and

Ionian sailors, and after pouring out a libation to Ea, the god of the sea, set sail from the mouth of the Euphrates. It was probably for the support of this fleet that the 20 talents (£10,800) annually levied on the district of Assur were intended. The Phœnician ships employed by the Assyrians were biremes, with two tiers of oars.

Of the Babylonian fleet we know but little. It does not seem to have taken part in the defence of the country at the time of the invasion of Cyrus. But the sailors who manned it were furnished with food, like the soldiers of the army, from the royal storehouse or granary. Thus in the sixteenth year of Nabonidos we have a memorandum to the effect that 210 *qas* of dates were sent from the storehouse in the month Tammuz "for the maintenance of the sailors." The King also kept a state-barge on the Euphrates, like the dahabias of Egypt. In the twenty-fourth year of Darius, for instance, a new barge was made for the monarch, two contractors undertaking to work upon it from the beginning of Iyyar, or April, to the end of Tisri, or September, and to use in its construction a particular kind of wood.

While we hear but little about the fleet, cargo and ferry-boats are frequently mentioned in letters and contracts. Reference has already been made to the shekel and a quarter paid by the agent of Belshazzar for the hire of a boat which conveyed three oxen and twenty-four sheep to the temple of the Sun-god at Sippara, in order that they might be sacrificed at the festival of the new year. Sixty *qas* of dates were at the same time given to the boatmen. In the reign of

Nebuchadnezzar, 3 shekels were paid for the hire of
a grain-boat, and in the thirty-sixth year of the same
King 4½ shekels were given for the hire of another
boat for the transport of wool.

Some documents translated by Mr. Pinches throw
light on the building and cost of the ships. One of
them is as follows : " A ship of six by the cubit beam,
twenty by the cubit the seat of its waters, which Nebo-
baladan, the son of Labasi, the son of Nur-Papsukal,
has sold to Sirikki, the son of Iddinâ, the son of
Egibi, for four manehs, ten shekels of silver, in one-
shekel pieces, which are not standard, and are in the
shape of a bird's tail (?). Nebo-baladan takes the
responsibility for the management (?) of the ship.
Nebo-baladan has received the money, four manehs
ten shekels of white (silver), the price of his ship, from
the hands of Sirikki." The contract, which was
signed by six witnesses, one of whom was "the King's
captain," was dated at Babylon in the twenty-sixth
year of Darius. Another contract relates to one of
the boats of the pontoon-bridge which ran across the
Euphrates and connected the two parts of Babylon together : " [Two] manehs ten shekels of white
(silver), coined in one-shekel pieces, not standard,
from Musezib, the son of Pisaram, to Sisku, the son
of Iddinâ, the son of Egibi. Musezibtum and Narum,
his female slaves—the wrist of Musezibtum is tattooed with the name of Iddinâ, the father of Sisku,
and the wrist of Narum is tattooed with the name of
Sisku—are the security of Musezib. There is no hire
paid for the slaves or interest on the money. Another possessor shall not have power over them until

Musezib receives the money, two manehs ten shekels
of white silver, in one-shekel pieces. Sisku, the son
of Iddinâ, takes the responsibility for the non-escape
of Musezibtum and Narum. The day when Musezibtum and Narum go elsewhere Sisku shall pay Musezib half a measure of grain a day by way of hire.
The money, which is for a ship for the bridge, has
been given to Sisku." This contract is also dated in
the twenty-sixth year of Darius.

A letter written in the time of Khammurabi, or
Amraphel, throws some light on the profits that were
made by conveying passengers. There were ships
which conveyed foreign merchants to Babylon if they
were furnished with passports allowing them to travel
and trade in the dominions of the Babylonian King.
They took their goods and commodities along with
them ; on one occasion, we are told, the boat in which
some of them travelled had been used for the conveyance of 10 talents of lead. It must, therefore, have
been of considerable size and draught.

That the army and navy should have been recruited
from abroad was in accordance with that spirit of lib-
erality toward the foreigner which had distinguished
the Babylonians from an early period. It was partly
due to the mixed character of the race, partly to the
early foundation of an empire which embraced the
greater portion of Western Asia, partly, and more especially, to the commercial instincts of the people.
We find among them none of that jealous exclusive-
ness which characterized most of the nations of antiquity. They were ready to receive into their midst
both the foreigner and his gods. Among Assyrian

and Babylonian officials we meet with many who bear
foreign names, and among the gods whose statues
found a place in the national temples of Assyria were
Khaldis of Armenia, and the divinities of the Bedâwin.
The policy of deporting a conquered nation was dic-
tated by the same readiness to admit the stranger to
the rights and privileges of a home-born native.   The
restrictions placed upon Babylonian and Assyrian
citizenship seem to have been but slight.

When Abraham was born at Ur of the Chaldees,
Babylonia was governed by a dynasty of South Arabian origin whose names had to be translated into the
Babylonian language.   Throughout the country there
were colonies of "Amorites," from Syria and Canaan,
doubtless established there for the purposes of trade,
who enjoyed the same rights as the native Babylonians.   They could hold and bequeath land and
other property, could buy and sell freely, could act
as witnesses in a case where natives alone were concerned, and could claim the full protection of Babylonian law.

One of these colonies, known as "the district of
the Amorites," was just outside the walls of Sippara.
In the reign of Ammi-zadok, the fourth successor of
Khammurabi, a dispute arose about the title to some
land included within it, and the matter was tried before the four royal judges.   The following record of
the judgment was drawn up by the clerk of the court :
"Twenty acres by thirteen of land in the district of
the Amorites which was purchased by Ibni-Hadad,
the merchant.   Arad-Sin, the son of Edirum, has
pleaded as follows before the judges : The building

land, along with the house of my father, he did
not buy; Ibku-Anunit and Dhab-Istar, the sons of
Samas-nazir, sold (it) for money to Ibni-Hadad, the
merchant. Iddatum and Mazitum, the sons of Ibni-
Hadad the merchant, appeared before the judges;
they lifted up (their hands) and swore that it had
been put up for sale; it had been bought by Edirum
and Sin-nadni-sû who handed it over to Samas-nazir
and Ibku-Anunit, selling it to them for money. The
estate, consisting of twenty-two acres of land enclosed
by thirty other acres, as well as eleven trees [and] a
house, in the district of the Amorites, bounded at the
upper end by the estate of ——, and at the lower end
by the river Bukai (?), is contracted in width, and is
of the aforesaid nature. Judgment has been given
for Arad-Sin, the son of Edirum, as follows: At the
entrance to Sippara the property is situated (?), and
after being put up for sale was bought by Samas-
nazir and Ibku-Anunit, to whom it was handed over;
power of redemption is allowed (?) to Arad-Sin; the
estate is there, let him take it. Before Uruki-mansum
the judge, Sin-ismeani the judge, Ibku-Anunit the
judge, and Ibku-ilisu the judge. The 6th day of the
month Tammuz, the year when Ammi-zadok the king
constructed the very great aqueduct (?) for the mountain and its fountain (?) for the house of Life."

If we may argue from the names, Arad-Sin, who
brought the action, was of Babylonian descent; and
in this case native Babylonians as well as foreigners
could hold land in the district in which the Amorites
had settled. At any rate, in the eyes of the law, the
native and the foreign settler must have been upon

an equal footing; they were tried before the same
judges, and the law which applied to the one applied
equally to the other. It is clear, moreover, that the
foreigner had as much right as the native to buy, sell,
or bequeath the soil of Babylonia.

Whether or not this right was restricted to particular districts, we do not know. In Syria, in later
days, "streets," or rows of shops in a city, could be
assigned to the members of another nationality by
special treaty, as we learn from 1 Kings xx. 34, and
at the end of the Egyptian eighteenth dynasty we
hear of a quarter at Memphis being given to a colony
of Hittite merchants, but such special assignments of
land may not have been the custom in ancient Chaldea. The Amorites of Canaan may have been allowed
to settle wherever they liked, and the origin of the
title "district of the Amorites" may have simply
been due to the tendency of foreign settlers to
establish themselves in the same locality. The fact
that Arad-Sin seems to have been a Babylonian, and
that his action was brought before Babylonian
judges, is in favor of the view that such was the
case.

Moreover, as Mr. Pinches has pointed out, Amorites
could rise to the highest offices of state. Not only
could they serve as witnesses to a deed, to which all
the other parties were native Babylonians, they could
also hold civil and military appointments. On the
one hand we find the son of Abi-ramu, or Abram, who
is described as "the father of the Amorite," acting
as a witness to a contract dated in the reign of the
grandfather of Khammurabi, or Amraphel ; on the

other hand, "an Amorite" has the same title of "servant" of the King as the royal judge Ibku-Anunit, and among the Assyrians of the second empire, who were slavish imitators of Babylonian custom and law, we meet with more than one example of a foreigner in the service of the Assyrian government. Thus, in the reign of Sargon, thirteen years after the fall of Samaria, the Israelites, Pekah and Nadabiah, who appear as witnesses to the sale of some slaves, are described, the one as "the governor of the city," the other as a departmental secretary. The founder, again, of one of the leading commercial families at Babylon under Nebuchadnezzar and his successors is entitled "the Egyptian," and the clerk who draws up a contract in the first year of Cambyses is the grandson of a Jew, Bel-Yahu, "Bel is Yahveh," while his father's name, Ae-nahid, "Ae is exalted," implies that the Israelitish Yahveh had been identified with the Babylonian Ae. Hebrew and Canaanite names appear in legal and commercial documents of the age of Khammurabi and earlier by the side of names of purely native stamp; Jacob-el and Joseph-el, for instance, Abdiel and Ishmael, come before us with all the rights and privileges of Babylonian citizens. The name of Ishmael, indeed, is already met with on a marble slab from Sippara, which is as early as about 4,000 B.C. In the time of Sargon of Akkad the Babylonian "governor" of Syria and Canaan bears the Canaanitish name of Uru-Malik, or Urimelech, and under the later Assyrian empire, the "tartan" of Comagene, with the Hittite name of Mar-lara, was an eponym, who gave his name to the year.

Mr. Pinches is probably right in seeing the name
" Israel " itself in that of a high-priest who lived in
the district of the Amorites outside Sippara in the
reign of Ammi-zadok. His name is written Sar-ilu,
and it was by his order that nine acres of ground " in
the district of the Amorites " were leased for a year
from two nuns, who were devotees of the Sun-god,
and their nieces. Six measures of grain on every ten
acres were to be paid to the Sun-god at the gate of
Malgia, the women themselves receiving a shekel of
silver as rent, and the field was to be handed back to
them at harvest-time, the end of the agricultural year.
That the women in the Amorite settlements enjoyed
the same freedom and powers as the women of Babylonia is shown by two documents, one dated in the
reign of the second King of the dynasty to which
Khammurabi belonged, the other in the reign of
Khammurabi's great-grandfather. In the first, Kuryatum, the daughter of an Amorite, receives a field of
more than four acres of which she had been wrongfully deprived ; in the second, the same Kuryatum
and her brother Sumu-rah are sued by the three children of an Amorite, one of whom is a woman, for the
recovery of a field, house, slaves, and date-palms.
The case was brought before " the judges of Bit-
Samas," " the Temple of the (Babylonian) Sun-god,"
who rejected the claim.

At a very early period of Babylonian history the
Syrian god Hadad, or Rimmon, had been, as it were,
domesticated in Babylonia, where he was known as
Amurru, " the Amorite." He had come with the
Amorite merchants and settlers, and was naturally

their patron-deity. His wife, Asratu, or Asherah, was called, by the Sumerians, Nin-Marki, " the mistress of the Amorite land," and was identified with their own Gubarra. Nin-Marki, or Asherah, presided over the Syrian settlements, the part of the city where the foreigners resided being under her protection like the gate which led to "the district of the Amorites" beyond the walls. The following lawsuit which came before the courts in the reign of Khammurabi shows that there were special judges for cases in which Amorites were concerned and that they sat at "the gate of Nin-Marki." " Concerning the garden of Sin-magir which Nahid-Amurri bought for money. Ilu-bani claimed it for the royal stables, and accordingly they went to the judges, and the judges sent them to the gate of Nin-Marki and the judges of the gate of Nin-Marki. In the gate of Nin-Marki Ilu-bani pleaded as follows : I am the son of Sin-magir; he adopted me as his son, and the seal of the document has never been broken. He further pleaded that ever since the reign of the deified Rim-Sin (Arioch) the garden and house had been adjudged to Ilu-bani. Then came Sin-mubalidh and claimed the garden of Ilu-bani, and they went to the judges and the judges pronounced that ' to us and the elders they have been sent and in the gate of the gods Merodach, Sussa, Nannar, Khusa, and Nin-Marki, the daughter of Merodach, in the judgment-hall, the disputants (?) have stood, and the elders before whom Nahid-Amurri first appeared in the gate of Nin-Marki have heard the declaration of Ilu-bani.' Accordingly they adjudged the garden and house to

Ilu-bani, forbidding Sin-mubalidh to return and claim
it. Oaths have been taken in the name of the Moon-
god, the Sun-god, Merodach, and Khammurabi, the
king. Before Sin-imguranni the president, Edilka-
Sin, Amil-izzitim, Ubarrum, Zanbil - arad - Sin, Ak-
hiya, Kabdu-gumi, Samas-bani, the son of Abia-rak-
has, Zanik-pisu, Izkur-Ea the steward, and Bauila.
The seals of the parties are attached. The fourth
day of Tammuz, the year when Khammurabi the
king offered up prayer to Tasmit."

While a portion of the land was thus owned by
foreigners, there was a considerable part of it which
belonged to the temples. Another part consisted of
royal domains, the revenue of which went to the
privy purse of the King. The King could make
grants of this to his favorites, or as a reward for
services to the state. The Babylonian King Nebo-
baladan, for example; gave one of his officials a field
large enough, it was calculated, to be sown with 3
gur of seed, and Assur-bani-pal of Assyria made his
vizier, Nebo-sar-uzur, the gift of a considerable estate on account of his loyalty from the time that the
King was a boy. All the vizier's lands, including
the serfs upon them, were declared free from taxation and every kind of burden, the men upon them
were not to be impressed as soldiers, nor the cattle
and flocks to be carried away. It was also ordered
that Nebo-sar-uzur, on his decease, should be buried
where he chose, and not in the common cemetery
outside the walls of the city. Like the monarch, he
might have his tomb in the royal palace or in his
own house, and imprecations were called down on

the head of anyone who wished to disturb his final resting-place. The deed of gift and privilege was sealed, we are told, with the King's own " signet-ring."

A grant of immunity from taxation and other burdens could be made to the inhabitants of a whole district. A deed exists, signed by a large number of witnesses, in which Nebuchadnezzar I. of Babylon (about 1200 B.C.) makes a grant of the kind to the district of Bit-Karziyabku in the mountains of Namri to the east of Babylonia. We read in it that, throughout the whole district, neither the royal messengers nor the governor of Namri shall have any jurisdiction, no horses, foals, mares, asses, oxen, or sheep shall be carried off by the tax-gatherers, no stallions shall be sent to the royal stables, and no taxes of grain and fruit shall be paid to the Babylonian treasury. Nor shall any of the inhabitants be impressed for military service. It speaks volumes for the commercial spirit of the Babylonians that a royal decree of this character should have been thrown into legal form, and that the names of witnesses should have been attached to it, just as if it had been a contract between two private persons. The contrast is striking with the decree issued by the Assyrian King, Assur-bani-pal, to his faithful servant Nebo-sar-uzur. All that was needed where the King of Assyria was concerned was his signet-seal and royal command. But Assur-bani-pal was an autocrat at the head of a military state. The Babylonian sovereign governed a commercial community and owed his authority to the priests of Bel.

CHAPTER IX

THE LAW

BABYLONIAN law was of early growth. Among the oldest records of the country are legal cases, abstracts of which have been transcribed for future use. The first law-book, in fact, was ascribed to Ea, the god of culture, and it was told how he had enacted that the King should deal uprightly and administer justice to his people. "If he regard not justice," it was said, "Ea, the god of destiny, shall change his fortune and replace him by another. . . . But if he have regard to the injunction of Ea, the great gods shall establish him in wisdom and the knowledge of righteousness."

The Ea of the cuneiform text seems to be the Oannes of the Chaldean historian Berossos, who was said to have risen out of the waters of the Persian Gulf, bringing with him the elements of civilization and the code of laws which were henceforth to prevail in Babylonia. The code of Oannes has perished, but fragments of another and more historical one have been preserved to us in a reading-book which was intended to teach the Semitic pupil the ancient language of the Sumerians. The original Sumerian text is given with its Semitic equivalent, as well as a list of technical legal terms. "If a son," it is said, "denies his father, his hair shall be cut, he shall be put into chains and sold for silver. If he denies his mother, his hair also shall be cut, city and land shall collect together and put him in prison. . . . If the wife hates her husband and denies him, they shall throw her into the river. If the husband divorces his wife, he must pay her fifty shekels of silver. If a man hires a servant, and kills, wounds, beats, or ill-uses him or makes him ill, he must with his own hand measure out for him each day half a measure of grain."

We have already seen that the last regulation was in force up to the latest period of Babylonian history. It betrays a humane spirit in the early legislation and shows that the slave was regarded as something more than a mere chattel. It provided against his being over-worked; as soon as the slave was rendered unfit for labor by his hirer's fault, the latter was fined, and the fine was exacted as long as the slave continued ill or maimed. The law which pronounced sentence of death by drowning upon the unfaithful wife was observed as late as the age of Khammurabi. Such at least is the evidence of some curious documents, from which we learn that a certain Arad-Samas married first a daughter of Uttatu and subsequently a half-sister of his wife. In the contract of marriage it is stipulated that unfaithfulness to the husband on the part of both the wives would be punished with drowning, on the part of the second only with slavery. On the other hand he could divorce them on payment of a maneh

of silver—that is to say, of 30 shekels apiece. Under
Nebuchadnezzar the old power of putting the wife to
death in case of adultery was still possessed by the
husband, where the wife was of lower rank than himself and little better than a concubine. It was a survival of the *patria potestas* which had once belonged
to him. The wife who came from a wealthy and
respectable family, however, stood on a footing of
equality with her husband, and he could not venture
to put in force against her the provisions of the
ancient Sumerian law.

Babylonian law resembled that of England in being
founded upon precedents. The code which was
supposed to have been revealed by Ea, or Oannes,
belonged to the infancy of Chaldean society and contained only a rudimentary system of legislation. The
actual law of the country was a complicated structure
which had been slowly built up by the labors of
generations. An abstract was made of every important case that came before the judges and of the
decision given in regard to it; these abstracts were
carefully preserved, and formed the basis of future
judgments.

The judges before whom the cases were brought
were appointed by the King, and acted in his place.
They sat under a president, and were usually four or
five in number. They had to sign their names at the
end of their judgments, after which the date of the
document was added. It is probable that they went
on circuit like Samuel in Israel and the "royal
judges " of Persia.

Where foreigners were involved the case was first

tried before special judges, who probably belonged to
the same nationality as the parties to the suit; if
one of the latter, however, was a Babylonian it was
afterward brought again before a native tribunal.
Sometimes in such cases the primitive custom was
retained of allowing "the elders" of the city to sit
along with the judges and pronounce upon the question in dispute.   They thus represented to a certain
extent an English jury.   Whether they appeared in
cases in which Babylonians alone were engaged is
doubtful.   We hear of them only where one at least
of the litigants is an Amorite from Canaan, and it is
therefore possible that their appearance was a con-
cession to Syrian custom.   In Babylonia they had
long been superseded by the judges, the royal power
having been greater there from the outset than in the
more democratic West, and consequently there would
have been but little need for their services.   If,
however, the foreign settlers had been accustomed at
home to have their disputes determined by a council
of elders, we can understand why they were still
allowed in Babylonia to plead before a similar tribunal, though it could do little more than second the
decisions of the judges.

Plaintiff and defendant pleaded their own causes,
which were drawn up in legal form by the clerks of
the court.   Witnesses were called and examined and
oaths were taken in the names of the gods and of the
King.

The King, it must be remembered, was in earlier times himself a god.   In later days the oaths
were usually dropped, and the evidence alone consid-

ered sufficient. Perhaps experience had taught the
bench that perjury was not a preventable crime.

Each case was tried by a select number of judges,
who were especially appointed to inquire into it, as
we may gather from a document dated at Babylon
the 6th day of Nisan in the seventeenth year of
Nebuchadnezzar. "[These are] the judges," it runs,
" before whom Sapik-zeri, the son of Zirutu, [and] Baladhu, the son of Nasikatum, the servant of the secretary of the Marshlands, have appeared in their suit
regarding a house. The house and deed had been
duly sealed by Zirutu, the father of Sapik-zeri, and
given to Baladhu. Baladhu, however, had come to
terms with Sapik-zeri and handed the house over to
him and had taken the deed (from the record-office)
and had given it to Sapik-zeri. Nebo-edher-napisti,
the prefect of the Marshlands; Nebo-suzzizanni, the
sub-prefect of the Marshlands; Merodach-erba, the
mayor of Erech; Imbi-ilu, the priest of Ur, Bel-
yuballidh, the son of Merodach-sum-ibni, the prefect
of the western bank; Abtâ, the son of Suzubu, the
son of Babutu; Musezib-Bel, the son of Nadin-akhi,
the son of the adopted one; Baniya, the son of
Abtâ, the priest of the temple of Sadu-rabu; and Samas-ibni, the priest of Sadu-rabu." The list of judges
shows that the civil governors could act as judges
and that the priests were also eligible for the post.
Neither the one class nor the other, however, is usually named, and we must conclude, therefore, that,
though the governor of a province or the mayor of a
town had a right to sit on the judicial bench, he did
not often avail himself of it.

The charge was drawn up in the technical form and attested by witnesses before it was presented to the court. We have an example of this dated at Sippara, the 28th day of Adar in the eighth year of Cyrus as King of Babylon: "Nebo-akhi-bullidh, the son of Su—, the governor of Sakhrin, on the 28th of Adar, the eighth year of Cyrus, king of Babylon and of the world, has brought the following charge against Bel-yuballidh, the priest of Sippara: I have taken Nanâ-iddin, son of Bau-eres, into my house because I am your father's brother and the governor of the city. Why, then, have you lifted up your hand against me? Rimmon-sar-uzur, the son of Nebo-yusezib; Nargiya and Erba, his brothers; Kutkah-ilu, the son of Bau-eres; Bel-yuballidh, the son of Bara-chiel; Bel-akhi-uzur, the son of Rimmon-yusallim; and Iqisa-abbu, the son of Samas-sar-uzur, have committed a crime by breaking through my door, entering into my house, and leaving it again after carrying away a maneh of silver." Then come the names of five witnesses and the clerk.

A suit might be compromised by the litigants before it came into court. In the reign of Nebuchadnezzar a certain Imliya brought witnesses to the door of the house of an official called Bel-iddin, and accused Arrali, the superintendent of the works, of having stolen an overcoat and a loin-cloth belonging to himself. But it was agreed that there would be no need on the part of the plaintiff to summon witnesses; the stolen goods were returned without recourse to the law.

The care taken not to convict without sufficient

evidence, and the thoroughness with which each case was investigated, is one of the most striking features in the records of the Babylonian lawsuits which have come down to us. Mention has already been made of the case of the runaway slave Barachiel, who pretended to be a free citizen and the adopted son of a Babylonian gentleman. Every effort seems to have been made to get at the truth, and some of the higher officials were associated with the judges before whom the matter was brought. Eventually cross-examination compelled Barachiel to confess the actual facts. It is noticeable that no torture was used to compel confession, even though the defendant was not a free citizen. No allusion, in fact, is ever made to torture, whether by the bastinado or otherwise ; the evidence of witnesses and the results of cross-examination are alone depended upon for arriving at the truth. In this respect the legal procedure of Babylonia offers an honorable contrast to that of ancient Greece or Rome, or even of Europe down to the middle of the last century.

Two cases which were pleaded before the courts in the reign of Nabonidos illustrate the carefulness with which the evidence was examined. One of them was a case of false witness. Beli-litu, the daughter of Bel-yusezib, the wine merchant (?), " gave the following testimony before the judges of Nabonidos, king of Babylon : In the month Ab, the first year of Nergal-sharezer, king of Babylon, I sold my slave Bazuzu for thirty-five shekels of silver to Nebo-akhi-iddin, the son of Sula of the family of Egibi, but he now asserts that I owed him a debt and so has not paid me the money. The judges heard the charge, and caused Nebo-akhi-iddin to be summoned and to appear before them. Nebo-akhi-iddin produced the contract which he had made with Beli-litu ; he proved that she had received the money, and convinced the judges. And Ziriya, Nebo-suma-lisir, and Edillu gave further testimony before the judges that Beli-litu, their mother, had received the silver." The judges deliberated and condemned Beli-litu to a fine of 55 shekels, the highest fine that could be inflicted on her, and then gave it to Nebo-akhi-iddin. It is possible that the prejudice which has always existed against the money-lender may have encouraged Beli-litu to commit her act of dishonesty and perjury. That the judges should have handed over the fine to the defendant, instead of paying it to the court or putting it into their own pockets, is somewhat remarkable in the history of law.

The second case is that of some Syrians who had settled in Babylonia and there been naturalized. The official abstract of it is as follows : " Bunanitum, the daughter of the Kharisian, brought the following complaint before the judges of Nabonidos, king of Babylon : Ben-Hadad-nathan, the son of Nikbaduh, married me and received three and one-half manehs of silver as my dowry, and I bore him a daughter. I and Ben-Hadad-nathan, my husband, traded with the money of my dowry, and we bought together a house standing on eight roods of ground, in the district on the west side of the Euphrates in the suburb of Borsippa, for nine and one-third manehs of silver, as

well as an additional two and one-half manehs, which
we received on loan without interest from Iddin-
Merodach, the son of Iqisa-ablu, the son of Nur-Sin,
and we invested it all in this house. In the fourth
year of Nabonidos, king of Babylon, I claimed my
dowry from my husband Ben-Hadad-nathan, and he
of his own free will gave me, under deed and seal,
the house in Borsippa and the eight roods on which
it stood, and assigned it to me for ever, stating in the
deed he gave me that the two and one-half manehs
which Ben-Hadad-nathan and Bunanitum had received from Iddin-Merodach and laid out in buying
this house had been their joint property. This deed
he sealed and called down in it the curse of the great
gods (upon whoever should violate it). In the fifth
year of Nabonidos, king of Babylon, I and my
husband, Ben-Hadad-nathan, adopted Ben-Hadad-
amara as our son and subscribed to the deed of
adoption, and at the same time we assigned two
manehs ten shekels of silver and the furniture of the
house as a dowry for my daughter Nubtâ. My
husband died, and now Aqabi-ilu (Jacob-el), the son
of my father-in-law, has raised a claim to the house
and property which was willed and assigned to
me, as well as (a claim) to Nebo-nur-ilani, whom we
bought for money through the agency of Nebo-
akhi-iddin.

I have brought him before you; pass judgment."
The judges heard their pleas; they read the deeds
and contracts which Bunanitum produced in court,
and disallowed the claim of Aqabi-ilu to the house in
Borsippa, which had been assigned to Bunanitum in

lieu of her dowry, as well as to Nebo-nur-ilani, whom
she and her husband had bought, and to the rest of
the property of Ben-Hadad-nathan ; they confirmed
Bunanitum and Ben-Hadad-amara in their titles.
(It was further added that) Iddin-Merodach should
receive in full the sum of two and one-half manehs
which he had given toward the purchase of the
house, and that then Bunanitum should take in full
three and one-half manehs, the amount of her dowry,
and that part of the property (which had not been
bequeathed to Nubtâ).   Nebo-nur-ilani was to be
given to Nubtâ in accordance with the will of her
father.   The following judges were present at the
delivery of this judgment: Nergal-banunu the judge,
the son of the architect; Nebo-akhi-iddin the judge,
the son of Egibi ; Nebo-sum-ukin the judge, the son
of Irani ; Bel-akhi-iddin the judge, the son of —— ;
Nebo-balasu-iqbi the judge, the son of —— ; and the
clerks Nadin and Nebo-sum-iskun.   Babylon, the
29th day of Elul, the ninth year of Nabonidos, king
of Babylon."

The term used in reference to the loan made by
Iddin-Merodach implies that the lender accepted a
share in the property that was bought instead of de-
manding interest for his money.   Hence it was that,
when the estate came to be settled after the death of
Ben-Hadad-nathan, it was necessary to pay him off.
What the grounds were upon which Aqabi-ilu laid
claim to the property we are not told, and the *dossier*
in which it was set forth has not been found.   His
name, however, is interesting, as it proves that the
old Western Semitic name of Jacob-el, of which the

Biblical Jacob is a shortened form, still survived in
a slightly changed shape among the Syrian settlers
in Babylonia. Indeed, Iqubu, or Jacob itself, is found
in a contract of the tenth year of Nabonidos as the
name of a coppersmith at Babylon. Two thousand
years before there had been other Semitic settlers in
Babylonia from Western Asia who had also taken
part in the legal transactions of the country, and
among whom the name of Ya'qub-ilu was known.
The name had even spread to the Assyrian colonists
near Kaisarîyeh, in Cappadocia, who have left us
inscriptions in uniform characters, and among them
it appears as Iqib-ilu. Iqib-ilu and Aqabi-ilu are
alike kindred forms of Ya'qub-ilu (or Yaqub-ilu), the
Jacob-el of Canaan.

Death, more especially with "an iron sword," was
the punishment of the more serious offences; imprisonment and scourging of lighter ones. Imprisonment
might be accompanied by chains or the stock, but the
prisoner might also be left unfettered and be allowed
to range freely through the court or cell of the prison.
Whether the penalty of imprisonment with hard labor
was ever inflicted is questionable; in a country where
slavery existed and the *corvée* was in force there would
have been but little need for it.

The prisoner could be released on bail, his surety
being responsible for his appearance when it was required. Thus in the seventh year of Cyrus one of
the officials of the temple of the Sun-god at Sippara
was put into "iron fetters" by the chief priest of the
god, but was afterward released, bail being given for
him by another official of the temple. The latter

undertook to do the work of the prisoner if he absconded. The bail was offered and accepted before
" the priests and elders of the city," and the registration of the fact was duly dated and attested by witnesses. At a later date a citizen of Nippur was allowed to become surety for the release of his nephew
from prison on condition that the latter did not leave
the city without permission. The prison is called
bit-karê, or " House of Walls." [1]

There was another *bit-karê*, which had a very different meaning and was used for a very different purpose. This was " the House of Cereals," the storehouse or barn in which were stored such tithes of the
temples as were paid in grain. The name is also
sometimes applied to the *sutumme*, or royal store-
houses, where the grain and dates collected by the
tax-gatherers were deposited, and from which the
army and the civil servants were provided with food.
The superintendent of these storehouses was an
important personage ; he was the paymaster of the
state officials, in so far as they received their salaries
in kind, and the loyalty of the standing army could
be trusted only so long as it could be fed. Similar
storehouses existed in Egypt, from the age of the
eighteenth dynasty downward, and it is probable that
the adoption of them was due to Babylonian influence. They gave the King a powerful hold upon his
subjects, by enabling him to supply them with grain
in the years of scarcity, or to withhold it except
upon such terms as he chose to make with them.

[1] In the Assyrian texts the term for " prison " is *bit kili*, of which
kisukku is also given as a synonym.

The exportation of the grain, moreover, was a yearly source of wealth and revenue which flowed into the royal exchequer. In Babylonia, as in Egypt, the controller of the granaries was master of the destinies of the people.

CHAPTER X

LETTER-WRITING

WE are apt to look upon letter-writing as a modern invention, some of us, perhaps, as a modern plague. But as a matter of fact it is an invention almost as old as civilization itself. As soon as man began to invent characters by means of which he could communicate his thoughts to others, he began to use them for holding intercourse with his absent friends. They took the place of the oral message, which was neither so confidential nor so safe. Classical scholars have long been familiar with the fact that letter-writing was one of the accomplishments of an educated Greek and Roman. The letters of Cicero and Pliny are famous, and the letters of Plato and Aristotle have been studied by a select few. Even Homer, who seems to avoid all reference to the art of writing as if it were an unclean thing, tells us of " the baleful characters " written on folded tablets, and sent by Prœtos to the King of Lycia. Criticism, it is true, not so long ago doubted the facts of the story and tried to resolve the characters and the tablets into a child's drawings on the slate. But archæology has come to the rescue of Prœtos, and while we now know that letters passed freely backward and forward

in the world in which he is supposed to have moved,
Mr. Arthur Evans has discovered the very symbols
which he is likely to have used. Even the Lycians,
to whom the letter was sent, have been found, not
only on the Egyptian monuments, but also in the tablets of Tel-el-Amarna.

Letter-writing in the East goes back to a remote
antiquity. In the book of Chronicles it is stated that
the messages that passed between Hiram and Solomon were in writing, but the age of Solomon was
modern when compared with that to which some of
the letters we now possess actually belong. Centuries earlier the words "message" and "letter" had
become synonymous terms, and in Hebrew the word
which had originally signified a "message" had come
to mean a "book." Not only is a message conceived
of as always written, but even the idea of a book is
taken from that of a letter. Nothing can show more
plainly the important place occupied by literary correspondence in the ancient Oriental world or the antiquity to which the art of the letter-writer reaches
back.

While in Egypt the letter was usually written upon
papyrus, in Western Asia the ordinary writing material was clay. Babylonia had been the nurse and
mother of its culture, and the writing material of
Babylonia was clay. Originally pictorial hieroglyph-
ics had been drawn upon the clay, but just as in
Egypt the hieratic or running-hand of the scribe
developed out of the primitive pictographs, so too in
Babylonia the pictures degenerated into cuneiform
characters which corresponded with the hieratic

characters of the Egyptian script. What we call cuneiform is essentially a cursive hand.

As for books, so also for letters the clay tablet was employed. It may seem to us indeed a somewhat cumbrous mode of sending a letter ; but it had the advantage of being solid and less likely to be injured or destroyed than other writing materials. The characters upon it could not be obliterated by a shower of rain, and there was no danger of its being torn. Moreover, it must be remembered that the tablet was usually of small size. The cuneiform system of writing allows a large number of words to be compressed into a small space, and the writing is generally so minute as to try the eyes of the modern decipherer.

Some of the letters which have been discovered during the last few years go back to the early days of the Babylonian monarchy. Many of them are dated in the reign of Khammurabi, or Amraphel, among them being several that were written by the King himself. That we should possess the autograph letters of a contemporary of Abraham is one of the romances of historical science, for it must be remembered that the letters are not copies, but the original documents themselves. What would not classical scholars give for the autograph originals of the letters of Cicero, or theologians for the actual manuscripts that were written by the Evangelists ? And yet here we have the private correspondence of a prince who took part in the campaign against Sodom and Gomorrah !

One of the letters which has found a resting-place in the Museum of Constantinople refers to another of the

actors in the campaign against the cities of the cunei-
plain. This was the King of Elam, Chedor-laomer,
whose name is written Kudur-Loghghamar in the
form. The Elamites had invaded Babylonia and
made it subject and tributary. Sin-idinnam, the King
of Larsa, called Ellasar in the book of Genesis, had
been compelled to fly from his ancestral kingdom in
the south of Chaldea, and take refuge in Babylon at
the court of Khammurabi. Eri-Aku, or Arioch, the
son of an Elamite prince, was placed on the throne
of Larsa, while Khammurabi also had to acknowledge
himself a vassal of the Elamite King. But a time
came when Khammurabi believed himself strong
enough to shake off the Elamite yoke, and though the
war at first seemed to go against him, he ultimately
succeeded in making himself independent. Arioch
and his Elamite allies were driven from Larsa, and
Babylon became the capital of a united monarchy.
It was after the overthrow of the Elamites that the
letter was written in which mention is made of Chedor-
laomer. Its discoverer, Père Scheil, gives the following
translation of it: "To Sin-idinnam, Khammurabi
says: I send you as a present (the images of) the
goddesses of the land of Emutalum as a reward for
your valor on the day of (the defeat of) Chedor-laomer.
If (the enemy) annoy you, destroy their forces with
the troops at your disposal, and let the images be restored in safety to their old habitations." [1]

---

[1] Our learned author has been misled in this paragraph by the
utterly erroneous copy and translation of Father Scheil. The letter reads " To Sin-iddinnam from Hammurabi. The goddesses of
Emutbalim which are assigned to thee, the troops under the com-

The letter was found at Senkereh, the ancient Larsa, where, doubtless, it had been treasured in the archive-chamber of the palace. Two other letters of Khammurabi, which are now at Constantinople, have also been translated by Dr. Scheil. One of them is as follows: "To Sin-idinnam, Khammurabi says : When you have seen this letter you will understand in regard to Amil-Samas and Nur-Nintu, the sons of Gisdubba, that if they are in Larsa, or in the territory of Larsa, you will order them to be sent away, and that one of your servants, on whom you can depend, shall take them and bring them to Babylon." The second letter relates to some officials about whom, it would seem, the King of Larsa had complained to his suzerain lord: " To Sin-idinnam, Khammurabi says: As to the officials who have resisted you in the accomplishment of their work, do not impose upon them any additional task, but oblige them to do what they ought to have performed, and then remove them from the influence of him who has brought them."

Long before the age of Khammurabi a royal post had been established in Babylon for the conveyance of letters. Fragments of clay had been found at Tello, bearing the impressions of seals belonging to the officials of Sargon of Akkad and his successor, and addressed to the viceroy of Lagas, to King Naram-Sin and other personages. They were, in fact, the envelopes of letters and despatches which passed between Lagas and Agadê, or Akkad, the capital of the dynasty.

mand of Tnuhsamar will bring to thee in safety. When they reach thee, with the troops which thou hast destroy the people, and the goddesses to their dwellings let them bring in safety."—CR.

Sometimes, however, the clay fragment has the form of a ball, and must then have been attached by a string to the missive like the seals of mediæval deeds. In either case the seal of the functionary from whom the missive came was imprinted upon it as well as the address of the person for whom it was intended. Thousands of letters seem to have passed to and fro in this manner, making it clear that the postal service of Babylonia was already well organized in the time of Sargon and Naram-Sin. The Tel-el-Amarna letters show that in the fifteenth century before our era a similar postal service was established throughout the Eastern world, from the banks of the Euphrates to those of the Nile. To what an antiquity it reached back it is at present impossible to say.

At all events, when Khammurabi was King, letters were frequent and common among the educated classes of the population. Most of those which have been preserved are from private individuals to one another, and consequently, though they tell us nothing about the political events of the time, they illustrate the social life of the period and prove how like it was to our own. One of them, for instance, describes the writer's journey to Elam and Arrapakhitis, while another relates to a ferry-boat and the boat-house in which it was kept. The boat-house, we are told, had fallen into decay in the reign of Khammurabi, and was sadly in want of repair, while the chief duty of the writer, who seems to have been the captain of the boat, was to convey the merchants who brought various commodities to Babylon. If the merchant, the letter states, was furnished with a royal passport, " we carried him across "

the river; if he had no passport, he was not allowed
to go to Babylon. Among other purposes for which
the vessel had been used was the conveyance of lead,
and it was capable of taking as much as 10 talents of
the metal. We further gather from the letter that it
was the custom to employ Bedâwin as messengers.

Among the early Babylonian documents found at
Sippara, and now in the Museum at Constantinople,
which have been published by Dr. Scheil, are two
private letters of the same age and similar character.
The first is as follows : " To my father, thus says
Zimri-eram : May the Sun-god and Merodach grant
thee everlasting life! May your health be good! I
write to ask you how you are ; send me back news of
your health. I am at present at Dur-Sin on the canal
of Bit-Sikir. In the place where I am living there is
nothing to be had for food. So I am sealing up and
sending you three-quarters of a silver shekel. In return for the money, send some good fish and other
provisions for me to eat." The second letter was despatched from Babylon, and runs thus : " To the lady
Kasbeya thus says Gimil-Merodach : May the Sun-
god and Merodach for my sake grant thee everlasting
life! I am writing to enquire after your health ;
please send me news of it. I am living at Babylon,
but have not seen you, which troubles me greatly.
Send me news of your coming to me, so that I may
be happy. Come in the month of Marchesvan (October). May you live for ever for my sake ! "

It is plain that the writer was in love with his cor-
respondent, and had grown impatient to see her again.
Both belonged to what we should call the professional

classes, and nothing can better illustrate how like in the matter of correspondence the age of Abraham was to our own. The old Babylonian's letter might easily have been written to-day, apart from the references to Merodach and the Sun-god. It must be noticed, moreover, that the lady to whom the letter is addressed is expected to reply to it. It is taken for granted that the ladies of Babylon could read and write as well as the men. This, however, is only what might have been concluded from the other facts of Babylonian social life, and the footing of equality with the man upon which the woman was placed in all matters of business. The fact that she could hold and bequeath property, and trade with it independently, implies that she was expected to know how to read and write. Even among the Tel-el-Amarna we find one or two from a lady who seems to have taken an active part in the politics of the day. "To the king my lord," she writes in one of them, "my gods, my Sun-god, thus says Nin, thy handmaid, the dust of thy feet. At the feet of the king my lord, my gods, my Sun-god, seven times seven I prostrate myself. Let the king my lord wrest his country from the hand of the Bedâwin, in order that they may not rob it. The city of Zaphon has been captured. This is for the information of the king my lord."

The letters of Tel-el-Amarna bridge over the gulf that separates the early Babylonia of Khammurabi from the later Assyria of Tiglath-pileser III. and his successors. The inner life of the intervening period is still known to us but imperfectly. No library or large collection of tablets belonging to it has as yet been discovered, and until this is the case we must remain less intimately acquainted with it than we are with the age of Khammurabi on the one hand, or that of the second Assyrian empire on the other.

It is true that the library of Nineveh, of which Assur-bani-pal was such a munificent patron, has preserved copies of some of the earlier epistolary literature of the country. Thus we have from it a fragment of a letter written by a King of Babylonia to two kings of Assyria, at a time when Assyria still acknowledged the supremacy of Babylon. But such documents are very rare, and apart from the Tel-el-Amarna tablets we have to descend to the days of the second Assyrian empire before we find again a collection of letters.

These are the letters addressed to the Assyrian government, or more generally to the King, in the reigns of Tiglath-pileser III., Shalmaneser IV., Sargon, Sennacherib, Esar-haddon, and Assur-bani-pal. They were preserved in the royal library of Nineveh, principally on account of their political and diplomatic importance, and are now in the British Museum. As might have been expected from their character, they throw more light on the politics of the day than on the social condition of the people. A few of them, however, are private communications to the King on other than political matters, and we also find among them reports in the form of letters from the royal astronomers, as well as upon such subjects as the importation of horses from Asia Minor for the royal stud. The letters have been copied by Professor R. F. Harper, who is now publishing them in a series of volumes. How numerous the letters are may be gathered from the fact that no less than 1,575 of them (including fragments) have come from that part of the library alone which was excavated by Sir A. H. Layard, and was the first to be brought to England.

Many of them are despatches from generals in the field or from the governors of frontier towns who write to inform the Assyrian government of the movements of the enemy or of the political events in their own neighborhood. It is from these letters, for example, that we learn the name of the King of Ararat who was the antagonist of Sennacherib and the predecessor of the King Erimenas, to whom his murderers fled for protection. The details, again, of the long Elamite war, which eventually laid Susa at the feet of Assyria, have been given us by them. It is needless, therefore, to insist upon the value they possess for the historian.

Among them, however, as has been already said, are some of a more private character. Here, for instance, is one which reminds us that human nature is much the same in all ages of the world: "To the king my lord, thy servant, Saul-miti-yuballidh: Salutation to the king my lord; may Nebo and Merodach for ever and ever be gracious to the king my lord. Bau-gamilat, the handmaid of the king, is constantly ill; she cannot eat a morsel of food; let the king send orders that some physician may go and see her." In another letter the writer expresses his gratitude to the King for his kindness in sending him his own doctor, who had cured him of a serious disease. "May Istar of Erech," he says, "and Nana (of Bit-

Ana) grant long life to the king my lord, for he sent
Basa the physician of the king my lord to save my life
and he has cured me ; therefore may the great gods of
heaven and earth be gracious to the king my lord, and
may they establish the throne of the king my lord in
heaven for ever ; since I was dead, and the king has
restored me to life." In fact there are a good many
letters which relate to medical matters.   Thus Dr.
Johnston gives the following translation of a letter
from a certain Arad-Nana, who seems to have been a
consulting physician, to Esar-haddon about a friend
of the prince who had suffered from violent bleeding
of the nose : " As regards the patient who has a bleeding from the nose, the Rab-Mag (or chief physician)
reports: 'Yesterday, toward evening, there was a
good deal of hæmorrhage.' The dressings have not
been properly applied.   They have been placed outside the nostrils, oppressing the breathing and coming off when there is hæmorrhage.   Let them be put
inside the nostrils and then the air will be excluded
and the hemorrhage stopped.   If it is agreeable to my
lord the king I will go to-morrow and give instruc-
tions; (meanwhile) let me know how the patient is."
Another letter from Arad-Nana translated by the
same Assyriologist is as follows: " To the king my
lord, thy servant Arad-Nana : May there be peace for
ever and ever to the king my lord.   May Ninip and
Gula grant health of soul and body to the king my
lord.   All is going on well with the poor fellow
whose eyes are diseased.   I had applied a dressing
covering the face.   Yesterday, toward evening, un-
doing the bandage which held it (in place), I removed

the dressing. There was pus upon the dressing, the size of the tip of the little finger. If any of your gods set his hand thereto, let him say so. Salutation for ever! Let the heart of the king my lord be rejoiced. Within seven or eight days the patient will recover."

The doctors were not alone in writing to the Assyrian King. Besides the reports which they were bound to make, the astronomers also sent letters to him on the results of their observations. Among the letters published by Professor Harper is an interesting one—unfortunately defaced and imperfect —which was sent to Nineveh from one of the observatories in Babylonia. After the ordinary compliments the writer, Abil-Istar, says: " As for the eclipse of the moon about which the king my lord has written to me, a watch was kept for it in the cities of Akkad, Borsippa, and Nippur. We observed it ourselves in the city of Akkad." Abil-Istar then goes on to describe the progress of the eclipse, but the lines are so broken as to be untranslatable, and when the text becomes perfect again we find him saying that he had written an exact report of the whole occurrence and sent it in a letter to the King. " And whereas the king my lord ordered me to observe also the eclipse of the sun, I watched to see whether it took place or not, and what passed before my eyes I now report to the king my lord. It was an eclipse of the moon that took place. . . It was total over Syria and the shadow fell on the land of the Amorites, the land of the Hittites, and in part on the land of the Chaldees." We gather from this let-

ter that there were no less than three observatories
in Northern Babylonia : one at Akkad, near Sippara;
one at Nippur, now Niffer; and one at Borsippa,
within sight of Babylon. As Borsippa possessed a
university, it was natural that one of the three observatories should be established there.

As nothing is said about the eclipse of the sun
which the astronomers at the Assyrian court had led
the King to expect, it is probable that it did not take
place, or at all events that it did not occur so soon as
was anticipated. The expression " the land of the
Amorites (and) the land of the Hittites " is noteworthy
on account of its biblical ring ; in the mind of the
Assyrian, however, it merely denoted Palestine and
Northern Syria. The Babylonians at an early age
called Palestine " the land of the Amorites," the
Assyrians termed it " the land of the Hittites," and
it would appear that in the days of the second Assyrian empire, when Babylonia had become a province of its Assyrian rival, the two names were com-
bined together in order to denote what we should
entitle " Syria."

Letters, however, were written to the King by all
sorts of people, and upon all sorts of business. Thus
we find Assur-bani, the captain of a river-barge, writing about the conveyance of some of those figures of
colossal bulls which adorned the entrance to the palace of Sennacherib. The letter is short and to the
point : " To the king my lord, thy servant Assur-bani :
Salutation to the king my lord. Assur-mukin has
ordered me to transport in boats the colossal bulls
and cherubim of stone. The boats are not strong

enough, and are not ready. But if a present be kindly made to us, we will see that they *are* got ready and ascend the river." The unblushing way in which *bakshish* is here demanded shows that in this respect, at all events, the East has changed but little.

Of quite a different character is a letter about some wine that was sent to the royal cellars. The writer says in it: " As for the wine about which the king my lord has written to me, there are two homers of it for keeping, as well as plenty of the best oil." Later on, in the same letter, reference is made to a *targumanu*, or " dragoman," who was sent along with the wine, which probably came from the Armenian highlands. It may be noted that in another letter mention is made of a " master of languages," who was employed in deciphering the despatches from Ararat.

A letter from the cellarers of the palace has been translated as follows by Dr. Johnston: " To the king our lord, thy servants . . . Bel-iqisa and Babilû: Salutation to the king our lord! May Assur, . . . Bel, and Nebo grant long life and everlasting years to the king our lord! Let the king our lord know that the wine received during the month Tebet has been bottled, but that there is no room for it, so we must make (new) cellars for the king our lord. Let the king our lord give orders that a (place for) the cellars be shown to us, and we shall be relieved from our embarrassment (?). The wine that has come for the king our lord is very considerable. Where shall we put it?"

A good deal of the correspondence relates to the

importation of horses from Eastern Asia Minor for the stables of the Assyrian King. The following is a specimen of what they are like: "To the king my lord, thy servant Nebo-sum-iddin: Salutation to the king my lord; for ever and ever may Nebo and Merodach be gracious to the king my lord. Thirteen horses from the land of Kusa, 3 foals from the land of Kusa—in all 16 draught-horses; 14 stallions; altogether 30 horses and 9 mules—in all 39 from the city of Qornê: 6 horses from the land of Kusa; 3 foals from Kusa—in all 9 draught-horses; 14 stallions; altogether 23 horses and 9 mules—in all 28 from the city of Dâna (Tyana): 19 horses of Kusa and 39 stallions—altogether 57 from the city of Kullania (Calneh); 25 stallions and 6 mules—in all 31 from the city of Arpad. All are gelded. Thirteen stallions and 10 mules—altogether 23 from the city of Isana. In all 54 horses from Kusa and 104 stallions, making 148 horses and 30 mules—altogether 177 have been imported. (Dated) the second day of Sivan."

The land of Kusa is elsewhere associated with the land of Mesa, which must also have lain to the north-west of Syria among the valleys of the Taurus. Kullania, which is mentioned as a city of Kusa, is the Calneh of the Old Testament, which Isaiah couples with Carchemish, and of which Amos says that it lay on the road to Hamath. The whole of this country, including the plains of Cilicia, has always been famous for horse-breeding, and one of the letters to the Assyrian King specially mentions Melid, the modern Malatiyeh, as exporting them to Nineveh.

Here the writer, after stating that he had "inscribed

in a register the number of horses " that had just arrived from Arrapakhitis, goes on to say : " What are the orders of the king about the horses which have arrived this very day before the king? Shall they be stabled in the garden-palace, or shall they be put out to grass? Let the king my lord send word whether they shall be put out to grass or whether they are to be stabled ? "

As is natural, several of the letters are upon religious matters. Among those which have been translated by Dr. Johnston there is one which throws light on the religious processions which were held in honor of the gods. " To the son of the king my lord, thy servant Nebo-sum-iddina : salutation to the son of the king my lord for ever and ever ! May Nebo and Merodach be gracious unto the son of the king my lord ! On the third day of the month Iyyar the city of Calah will consecrate the couch of Nebo, and the god will enter the bed-chamber. On the fourth day Nebo will return. The son of the king my lord has (now) received the news. I am the governor of the temple of Nebo thy god, and will (therefore) go. At Calah the God will come forth from the interior of the palace, (and) from the interior of the palace will go to the grove. A sacrifice will be offered. The charioteer of the gods will go from the stable of the gods, will take the god out of it, will carry him in procession and bring him back. This is the course of the procession. Of the vase-bearers, whoever has a sacrifice to make will offer it. Whoever offers up one *qa* of his food may enter the temple of Nebo. May the offerers fully accomplish the ordinances of

the gods, to the life and health of the son of the king
my lord. What (commands) has the son of the king
my lord to send me? May Bel and Nebo, who granted
help in the month Sebat, protect the life of the son of
the king my lord, and cause thy sovereignty to continue to the end of time!"

There is another letter in which, if Dr. Johnston's
rendering is correct, reference is made to the inscriptions that were written on the walls of the temples like
the texts which the book of Deuteronomy orders to
be inscribed on the door-posts and gates (Deut. vi. 9,
and xi. 20). "To the king my lord, thy servant Istar-
Turi: salutation to the king my lord! I am sending
Nebo-sum-iddina and Nebo-erba, the physicians of
whom I spoke to the king, [with] my messenger to
the presence of the king my lord. Let them be admitted to the presence of the king my lord; let the
king my lord converse with them. I have not dis-
closed to them the real facts, and tell them nothing.
As the king my lord commands, so is it done. Samas-
bel-utsur sends word from the city of Der that ' there
are no inscriptions which we can place on the walls
of the Beth-el.' I send accordingly to the king my
lord in order that an inscription may be written and
despatched, (and) that the rest may be soon written
and placed on the walls of the Beth-el. There has
been a great deal of rain, (but) the harvest is gathered.
May the heart of the king my lord rejoice!"

While the letters which have been found on the
site of Nineveh come from the royal archives and are
therefore with few exceptions addressed to the King,
those which have been discovered in Babylonia have

more usually been sent by one private individual to another. They represent for the most part the private correspondence of the country, and prove how widely education must have been diffused there. Most of them, moreover, belong to the age of Khammurabi or that of the kings of Ur who preceded the dynasty to which he belonged, and thus cast an unexpected light on the life of the Babylonian community in the times of Abraham. Here, for example, is one that was written by a tenant to his landlord : "To my lord says Ibgatum, your servant. As, my lord, you have heard, an enemy has carried away my oxen. Though I never before wrote to you, my lord, now I send this letter (*literally* tablet). O my lord, send me a cow ! I will lie up five shekels of silver and send them to my lord, even to you. O my lord, by the command of Merodach you determine whatever place you prefer (to be in) ; no one can hinder you, my lord. O my lord, as I will send you by night the five shekels of silver which I am tying up, so do you put them away at night. O my lord, grant my request and do glorify my head, and in the sight of my brethren my head shall not be humbled. As to what I send you, O my lord, my lord will not be angry (?). I am your servant ; your wishes, O my lord, I have performed superabundantly ; therefore entrust me with the cow which you, my lord, shall send,`and in the town of Uru-Batsu your name, O my lord, shall be celebrated for ever. If you, my lord, will grant me this favor, send [the cow] with Ili-ikisam my brother, and let it come, and I will work diligently at the business of my lord, if he will send the cow. I

am tying up the five shekels of silver and am
sending them in all haste to you, my lord."

Ibgatum was evidently the lessee of a farm, and
he does his best to get a cow out of his landlord in
order to make up for the loss of his oxen. The 5
shekels probably represented the rent due to the
landlord, and his promptitude in sending them was
one of the arguments he used to get the cow. The
word rendered "tie up" means literally "to yoke,'
so that the shekels would appear to have been in the
form of rings rather than bars of metal.

A letter in the collection of Sir Henry Peck, which
has been translated by Mr. Pinches, is addressed to
the landlord by his agent or factor, whose duty it was
to look after his country estates. It runs as follows :
"Letter from Daian-bel-ussur to Sirku my lord. I
pray to-day to Bel and Nebo for the preservation of
the life of my lord. As regards the oxen which my
lord has sent, Bel and Nebo know that there is an
ox [among them] for them from thee. I have made
the irrigation-channel and wall. I have seen thy
servant with the sheep, and thy servant with the
oxen ; order also that an ox may be brought up thence
[as an offering?] unto Nebo, for I have not purchased a single ox for money. I saw fifty-six of them
on the 20th day, when I offered sacrifice to Samas.
I have caused twenty head to be sent from his hands
to my lord. As for the garlic, which my lord bought
from the governor, the owner of the field took possession of it when [the sellers] had gone away, and
the governor of the district sold it for silver ; so the
plantations also I am guarding there [?], and my

lord has asked: Why hast thou not sent my messenger and [why] hast thou measured the ground?
about this also I send thee word. Let a messenger
take and deliver [?] thy message."

Another letter of the same age is interesting as
showing that the name of the national God of Israel,
Yahum or Yahveh, was known in Babylonia at a
much earlier date than has hitherto been suspected:
" To Igas-Nin-sagh thus says Yahum-ilu: As thou
knowest, Adâ-ilu has obtained for me the money
. . . for the maid-servant Khisam-ezib. Mida [?]
the merchant has settled the price with me [?]. Now
let the notary of Babylon send Arad-Istar in . . . ,
the three shekels of silver which you have in hand
and the two shekels which you have put out at interest, and I will straightway bring the money [and]
Arad-Istar. Do not hinder Arad-Istar and I will
straightway bring him to the government."

Yahum-ilu is the Joel of the Old Testament, with
the final *m* which distinguished the languages of early
Babylonia and Southern Arabia, and the name probably belonged to one of those " Amorites " or natives
of Syria and Palestine who were settled in Babylonia.
Yahum-ilu, however, might also have been a native
of Southern Arabia. The important fact is the occurrence of the name at so early a date.

That the clay tablet should ever have been used
for epistolary purposes seems strange to us who are
accustomed to paper and envelopes. But it occupied
no more space than many modern official letters, and
was lighter to carry than most of the packages that
pass through the parcel-post. Now and then it was

enveloped in an outer covering of clay, on which the
address and the chief contents of it were noted ; but
the public were usually prevented from knowing what
it contained in another way. Before it was handed
over to the messenger or postman it was " sealed,"
which generally appears to mean that it was deposited in some receptacle, perhaps of leather or
linen, which was then tied up and sealed. In fact,
Babylonian and Assyrian letters were treated much as
ours are when they are put into a post-bag to which
the seals of the post-office are attached. There were
excellent roads all over Western Asia, with post-
stations at intervals where relays of horses could be
procured. Along these all letters to or from the King
and the government were carried by royal messengers. It is probable that the letters of private individuals were also carried by the same hands.

The letters of Tel-el-Amarna give us some idea of
the wide extension of the postal system and the ease
with which letters were constantly being conveyed
from one part of the East to another. The foreign
correspondence of the Pharaoh was carried on with
Babylonia and Assyria in the east, Mesopotamia and
Cappadocia in the north, and Palestine and Syria in
the west. The civilized and Oriental world was thus
bound together by a network of postal routes over
which literary intercourse was perpetually passing.
They extended from the Euphrates to the Nile and
from the plateau of Asia Minor to the confines of
Arabia. These routes followed the old lines of war
and trade along which armies had marched and merchants had travelled for unnumbered generations.

The Tel-el-Amarna tablets show us that letter-writing was not confined to Assyria and Babylonia on the one hand, or to Egypt on the other. Wherever the ancient culture of Babylonia had spread, there had gone with it not only the cuneiform characters and the use of clay as a writing material, but the art of letter-writing as well. The Canaanite corresponded with his friends and neighbors quite as much as the Babylonian, and his correspondence was conducted in the same language and script. Hiram of Tyre, in sending letters to Solomon, did but carry on the traditions of a distant past. Long before the Israelites entered Palestine both a foreign and an inland postal service had been established there while it was still under Babylonian rule. The art of reading and writing must have been widely spread, and, when it is remembered that for the larger number of the Tel-el-Amarna writers the language and system of writing which they used were of foreign origin, it may be concluded that the education given at the time was of no despicable character.

The same conclusion may be drawn from another fact. The spelling of the Babylonian and Assyrian letters is in general extraordinarily correct. We meet, of course, with numerous colloquialisms which do not occur in the literary texts, and now and then with provincial expressions, but it is seldom that a word is incorrectly written. Even in the Tel-el-Amarna tablets, where all kinds of local pronunciation are reproduced, the orthography is usually faultless, in spite of the phonetic spelling. All this shows how carefully the writers must have been instructed at school. The correctness of the spelling in the Assyrian letters is really marvellous, especially when we consider all the difficulties of the cuneiform script, and what a tax it must have been to the memory to remember the multitudinous characters of the syllabary with their still more multitudinous phonetic and ideographic values. It gives us a high idea of the perfection to which the teachers' art had already been brought.

In Assyria, however, the writers usually belonged to the special class of scribes who employed the same conventional hand and devoted their lives to the acquisition of learning. It is probable that they acted as private secretaries as well as public clerks, and that consequently many of the letters which purport to come from other members of the community were really written by the professional scribes. But in Babylonia it is difficult to find any traces of the public or private letter-writer who is still so conspicuous a figure in the East. It is seldom if ever that the Babylonian, whoever he may be, betrays any ignorance of the art of reading and writing, and the endless variety of handwritings and the execrable character of many of them indicate pretty plainly that the aid of the professional letter-writer was rarely invoked. In a commercial community like that of Babylonia an ability to write was of necessity a matter of primary importance.

CHAPTER XI

RELIGION

As in other countries, so too in Babylonia, the official and the popular religion were not in all respects the same. In the popular faith older superstitions and beliefs still lingered which had disappeared from the religion of the state or appeared in it in another form. The place of the priest was in large measure taken by the sorcerer and the magician, the ceremonies of the public cult were superseded by charms and incantations, and the deities of the official creed were overshadowed by a crowd of subordinate spirits whose very existence was hardly recognized among the more cultured classes. The Babylonian was inordinately superstitious, and superstition naturally flourished most where education was least.

The official creed itself was an artificial amalgamation of two different currents of belief. The Babylonian race was mixed; Sumerian and Semite had gone to form it in days before history began. Its religion, therefore, was equally mixed; the religious conceptions of the Sumerian and the Semite differed widely, and it was the absorption of the Sumerian element by the Semitic which created the religion of later days. It is Semitic in its general character, but in its general character alone. In details it resembles the religions of the other Semitic nations of Western Asia only in so far as they have been influenced by it.

The Sumerian had no conception of what we mean by a god. The supernatural powers he worshipped or feared were spirits of a material nature. Every object had its zi, or "spirit," which accompanied it like a shadow, but unlike a shadow could act independently of the object to which it belonged. The forces and phenomena of nature were themselves "spirits;" the lightning which struck the temple, or the heat which parched up the vegetation of spring, were as much "spirits" as the zi, or "spirit," which enabled the arrow to reach its mark and to slay its victim. When contact with the Semites had introduced the idea of a god among the Sumerians, it was still under the form of a spirit that their powers and attributes were conceived. The Sumerian who had been unaffected by Semitic teaching spoke of the "spirit of heaven" rather than of the god or goddess of the sky, of the "spirit of Ea" rather than of Ea himself, the god of the deep. Man, too, had a zi, or "spirit," attached to him; it was the life which gave him movement and feeling, the principle of vitality which constituted his individual existence. In fact, it was the display of vital energy in man and the lower animals from which the whole conception of the zi was derived. The force which enables the animate being to breathe and act, to move and feel, was extended to inanimate objects as well; if the sun and stars moved through the heavens, or the arrow flew through the air, it was from the same cause as that which enabled the man to walk or the bird to fly.

The *zi* of the Sumerians was thus a counterpart of the *ka*, or "double," of Egyptian belief. The description given by Egyptian students of the *ka* would apply equally to the *zi* of Sumerian belief. They both belong to the same level of religious thought; indeed, so closely do they resemble one another that the question arises whether the Egyptian belief was not derived from that of ancient Sumer.

Wholly different was the idea which underlay the Semitic conception of a spiritual world. He believed in a god in whose image man had been made. It was a god whose attributes were human, but intensified in power and action. The human family on earth had its counterpart in the divine family in heaven. By the side of the god stood the goddess, a colorless reflection of the god, like the woman by the side of the man. The divine pair were accompanied by a son, the heir to his father's power and his representative and interpreter. As man stood at the head of created things in this world, so, too, the god stood at the head of all creation. He had called all things into existence, and could destroy them if he chose.

The Semite addressed his god as Baal or Bel, "the lord." It was the same title as that which was given to the head of the family, by the wife to the husband, by the servant to his master. There were as many Baalim or Baals as there were groups of worshippers. Each family, each clan, and each tribe had its own Baal, and when families and clans developed into

cities and states the Baalim developed along with
them. The visible form of Baal was the Sun; the
Sun was lord of heaven and therewith of the earth
also and all that was upon it. But the Sun presented
itself under two aspects. On the one side it was the
source of light and life, ripening the grain and bringing the herb into blossom; on the other hand it
parched all living things with the fierce heats of summer and destroyed what it had brought into being.
Baal, the Sun-god, was thus at once beneficent and
malevolent; at times he looked favorably upon his
adorers, at other times he was full of anger and sent
plague and misfortune upon them. But under both
aspects he was essentially a god of nature, and the
rites with which he was worshipped accordingly were
sensuous and even sensual.

Such were the two utterly dissimilar conceptions of
the divine out of the union of which the official religion of Babylonia was formed. The popular religion
of the country also grew out of them though in a more
unconscious way. The Semite gave the Sumerian
his gods with their priests and temples and ceremonies. The Sumerian gave in return his belief in a
multitude of spirits, his charms and necromancy, his
sorcerers and their sacred books.

Unlike the gods of the Semites, the "spirits" of the
Sumerian were not moved by human passions. They
had, in fact, no moral nature. Like the objects and
forces they represented, they surrounded mankind,
upon whom they would inflict injury or confer benefits.
But the injuries were more frequent than the benefits; the sum of suffering and evil exceeds that of hap-

piness in this world, more especially in a primitive condition of society. Hence the "spirits" were feared
as demons rather than worshipped as powers of
good, and instead of a priest a sorcerer was needed
who knew the charms and incantations which could
avert their malevolence or compel them to be serviceable to men. Sumerian religion, in fact, was Shamanistic, like that of some Siberian tribes to-day, and its
ministers were Shamans or medicine-men skilled in
witchcraft and sorcery whose spells were potent to
parry the attacks of the demon and drive him from
the body of his victim, or to call him down in ven-
geance on the person of their enemy.

Shamanism, however, pure and simple, is incom-
patible with an advanced state of culture, and as time
went on the Shamanistic faith of the Sumerians tended
toward a rudimentary form of polytheism. Out of
the multitude of spirits there were two or three who
assumed a more commanding position than the rest.
The spirit of the sky, the spirit of the water, and
more especially the spirit of the underground world,
where the ghosts of the dead and the demons of
night congregated together, took precedence of the
rest. Already, before contact with the Semites, they
began to assume the attributes of gods. Temples
were raised in their honor, and where there were temples there were also priests.

This transition of certain spirits into gods seems
to have been aided by that study of the heavens and
of the heavenly bodies for which the Babylonians
were immemorially famous. At all events, the ideograph which denotes "a god" is an eight-rayed star,

from which we may perhaps infer that, at the time of the invention of the picture-writing out of which the cuneiform characters grew, the gods and the stars were identical.

One of the oldest of the Sumerian temples was that of Nippur, the modern Niffer, built in honor of Mul-lil or El-lil, "the lord of the ghost-world." He had originally been the spirit of the earth and the underground world; when he became a god his old attributes still clung to him. To the last he was the ruler of the *lil-mes*, "the ghosts" and "demons" who dwelt in the air and the waste places of the earth, as well as in the abode of death and darkness that lay beneath it. His priests preserved their old Shamanistic character; the ritual they celebrated was one of spells and incantations, of magical rites and ceremonies. Nippur was the source and centre of one of the two great streams of religious thought and culture which influenced Sumerian Babylonia.

The other source and centre was Eridu on the Persian Gulf. Here the spirit of the water was worshipped, who in process of time passed into Ea, the god of the deep. But the deep was a channel for foreign culture and foreign ideas. Maritime trade brought the natives of Eridu into contact with the populations of other lands, and introduced new religious conceptions which intermingled with those of the Sumerians. Ea, the patron deity of Eridu, became the god of culture and light, who delighted in doing good to mankind and in bestowing upon them the gifts of civilization. In this he was aided by his son Asari, who was at once the interpreter of his will and

the healer of men. His office was declared in the
title that was given to him of the god "who benefits
mankind."

Two strongly contrasted streams of religious influence thus flowed from Nippur in the north of Babylonia and from Eridu in the south. The one brought
with it a belief in the powers of darkness and evil,
in sorcery and magic, and a religion of fear; the other
spoke of light and culture, of gods who poured bless-
ings upon men and healed the diseases that afflicted
them. Asari was addressed as "he who raises the
dead to life," and Ea was held to be the first legis-
lator and creator of civilized society.

How far the foreign influence which moulded the
creed of Eridu was of Semitic origin it is impossible
to say. Semitic influences, however, began to work
upon Sumerian religion at a very early date. The
Semite and the Sumerian intermingled with one
another; at first the Semite received the elements of
culture from his more civilized neighbor, but a time
came when he began to give something in return.
The result of this introduction of Semitic and Sumerian beliefs and ideas was the official religion of
later Babylonia.

The "spirits" who had ranked above the rest now
became gods in the Semitic sense of the term. Mul-
lil of Nippur became the Semitic Baal or Bel, the
supreme lord of the world, who governs the world
below as well as the world above. He it was who
conferred empire over mankind upon his worshippers
and whose ministers and angels were the spirits of
popular belief. Ea wanted but little to become a

true god ; his name remained unchanged and his dominion extended to all waters whatever, wherever they might be. His son Asari passed into Merodach, the patron-deity of Babylon, who, when his city became the capital of Babylonia, took the place of Bel of Nippur as the supreme Bel. As in Greek mythology the younger Zeus dethroned his father, so in Babylonia the younger Bel of Babylonia dethroned the older Bel of Nippur.

Similarly, Anu, the spirit of the sky, became the Semitic Sky-god Anu, whose temple stood at Erech. Ur, on the western bank of the Euphrates, was dedicated to the Moon-god under the name of Sin, like Harran in Mesopotamia ; Larsa was dedicated to the Sun-god. When Borsippa became a suburb of Babylon its presiding deity became at the same time the minister and interpreter of Merodach under the title of Nabium or Nebo "the prophet." The Semitic god everywhere took the place of the Sumerian "spirit," while those among the "spirits" themselves who had not undergone the transforming process merged in the three hundred spirits of heaven and the six hundred spirits of earth. They formed the "hosts of heaven," of whom Bel was the lord.

But Semitic belief necessitated the existence of a goddess by the side of the god. It was, indeed, a grammatical necessity rather than a theological one ; the noun in the Semitic languages has a feminine as well as a masculine gender, and the masculine Bilu or Bel, accordingly, implied a female Belit or Beltis. But the goddess was little more than a grammatical shadow of the god, and her position was still further weak-

ened by the analogy of the human family where the
wife was regarded as the lesser man, the slave and
helpmeet of her husband.

One goddess only escaped the general law which
would have made her merely the pale reflection of
the god. This was Istar. Istar was an independent
deity, owing no allegiance to a husband, and standing on a footing of equality with the gods. But this
was because she had once been one of the chief objects of Sumerian worship, the spirit of the evening
star. In the Sumerian language there was no gender,
nothing that could distinguish the goddess or the
woman from the god or man, and the "spirits," therefore, were indifferently of both sexes. Moreover, the
woman occupied an important place in the Sumerian family; where the Semitic translation speaks of
"man and woman" the Sumerian original makes it
"woman and man." To the Sumerian mind, accordingly, the female "spirit" was as powerful as the
male, acting independently and possessing the same
attributes. Hence it was that in taking Istar over
from their Sumerian predecessors the Semitic inhabitants of Babylonia took over at the same time a
goddess who was the equal of a god.

Among the mixed population of Babylonia, with
its mixed culture and language and religion, the
character and position of Istar underwent but little
change. But when the conquerors of Sargon of
Akkad and his predecessors carried the civilization
of Babylonia to the West, Istar assumed a new form.
Among the Canaanites she became Ashtoreth with the
feminine termination, and was identified with the

Moon, the consort and reflection, as it were, of Baal
the Sun-god. But even so, the existence, of an independent goddess by the side of Baal seemed
strange to the Semitic imagination, and among the
Semites of Southern Arabia she was transformed into
a male god, while the Moabites made her one with
the god Chemosh. Even among the learned classes
of Semitic Babylonia it was whispered that she was
of both sexes, a goddess when imaged in the evening
star, a god when visible in the star of the morning.

Closely connected with the worship of Istar was
that of Tammuz. Tammuz among the Sumerians
appears to have been the "spirit" of the rivulets and
waters of spring, and his name signified literally
"the son of life" or "of the spirit." But among
the Semites he became the young and beautiful
shepherd, the beloved of Istar, slain by the boar's
tusk of winter, or, as others held, of the parching
heats of the summer. He symbolized the fresh vegetation of the spring and the Sun-god who called it
forth. Once each year, in the sultry heats of June,
the women wept and tore their hair in memory of
his untimely death, and Istar, it was said, had descended into Hades in the vain hope of bringing him
back to life. One of the most famous of Babylonian
poems was that which told of the descent of Istar
through the seven gates of the underground world,
and which was chanted at the annual commemoration
of his death. At each gate, it is said, the goddess
left behind her some one of her adornments, until at
last she arrived stripped and naked before the throne
of the goddess of the infernal world. The poem was

composed at a time when astronomical conceptions
had laid hold of the old mythology, and the poet has
interwoven the story of the waning and waxing of the
moon into the ancient tale.

The world was generally believed to have originated out of a watery chaos, and to float, as it were,
upon the deep. This belief was derived from Eridu,
where it was also taught that the deep surrounded
the earth like the coils of a serpent.

But other ideas about the origin of things prevailed elsewhere. Inland it was supposed that the
firmament of heaven rested on the peak of a mountain—"the mountain of the East," or "of the World,"
as it was commonly called—where the gods lived in
an Olympus of their own and the stars were sus-
pended from it like lamps. The firmament was regarded as a kind of extinguisher or as the upturned
hull of one of the round coracles that plied on the
Euphrates. Other ideas again were prevalent in
other parts of the country. Thus at Eridu the place
of "the mountain of the World" was taken by a magical tree which grew in the midst of the garden of
Eden, or "plain" of Babylonia, and on either side
of which were the mouths of the Tigris and Euphrates. It is probably to be identified with the tree
of life which figures so frequently in the sculptures
of Assyria and on the seal-cylinders of Chaldea, but
it may be the tree of knowledge of which we hear in
the old Sumerian texts, and upon which "the name
of Ea was written." At all events it is "the holy
tree of Eridu," of whose "oracle" Arioch calls himself "the executor."

The sun, it was believed, rose and set from between the twin mountains whose gates were guarded
by men with the bodies of scorpions, while their
heads touched the skies and their feet reached to
Hades. The scorpion was the inhabitant of the desert of Northern Arabia, the land of Mas, where the
mountains of the sunset were imagined to be. Beyond them were the encircling ocean and the waters
of Death, and beyond these again the island of the
Blest, where the favorites of the gods were permitted
to dwell. It was hither that Xisuthros, the Chaldean
Noah, was translated for his piety after the Deluge,
and it was here, too, that the flower of immortality
blossomed.

For the ordinary mortal a very different fate was
reserved. He had to descend after death into the
underground world of Hades, where the spirits of the
dead flitted about like bats in the darkness, with
dust only for their food. It was a land of gloom and
forgetfulness, defended by seven gates and seven
warders, who prevented the dead from breaking forth
from their prison-house and devouring the living under the form of vampires. The goddess Allat presided over it, keeping watch over the waters of life
that bubbled up under her golden throne. Before
her sat the shades of the heroes of old, each crowned
with a shadowy crown and seated on a shadowy
throne, rising up only that they might salute the
ghost of some human potentate who came to join
them from the upper world. In later days, it is true,
brighter and higher conceptions of the after life came
to prevail, and an Assyrian poet prays that his King,

when he dies, may pass away to "the land of the silver sky."

The various cosmological speculations and beliefs of ancient Chaldea were collected together in later times and an attempt made to combine them into a philosophical system. What this was like we learn from the opening lines of the epic which recounted the story of the Creation. In the beginning, we are told, was the chaos of the deep, which was the mother of all things. Out of it came first the primeval gods, Lakhum and Lakhamu, whose names had been handed down from the Sumerian age. Then came An-sar and Ki-sar, the Upper and Lower Firmaments, and, lastly, the great gods of the Semitic faith, Anu, Bel of Nippur, and Ea. All was ready at last for the creation of the present heavens and earth. But a struggle had first to be carried on between the new gods of light and order and Tiamat, the dragon of the "Deep," the impersonation of chaos. Merodach volunteered the task; Tiamat and her demoniac allies were overthrown and the sky formed out of her skin, while her blood became the rivers and springs. The deep was placed under fetters, that it might never again break forth and reduce the world to primeval chaos; laws were laid down for the heavenly bodies, which they were to keep forever and so provide a measure of time, and the plants and animals of the earth were created, with man at the head to rule over them. Though man was made of the dust, he was, nevertheless, the "son" of the gods, whose outward forms were the same as his.

It is not to be supposed that this philosophizing

of the old myths and legends made its way beyond
the circle of the learned classes, but the myths and
legends themselves were known to the people and
served instead of a cosmology. The struggle between Tiamat and Merodach was depicted on the
walls of the temple of Bel at Babylon, and the belief that this world has arisen out of a victory of order over chaos and anarchy was deeply implanted
in the mind of the Babylonian. Perhaps it goes
back to the time when the soil of Babylonia was won
by the cultivator and the engineer from wild and un-
restrained nature.

Babylonian religion had its sacred books, and, like
the official cosmology, a real knowledge of them was
probably confined to the priests and educated classes.
But a considerable part of their contents must have
been more widely known.

Some of the hymns embodied in them, as well as
the incantations and magical ceremonies, were doubtless familiar to the people or derived from current
superstitions. The work in which the hymns were
collected and procured, and which has been compared
with the Veda of India, was at once the Bible and
the Prayer-book of Chaldea. The hymns were in
Sumerian, which thus became a sacred language, and
any mistake in the recitation of them was held to be
fatal to the validity of a religious rite. Not only,
therefore, were the hymns provided with a Semitic
translation, but from time to time directions were
added regarding the pronunciation of certain words.
The bulk of the hymns was of Sumerian origin, but
many new hymns, chiefly in honor of the Sun-god,

had been added to them in Semitic times. They
were, however, written in the old language of Sumer;
like Latin in the Roman Catholic Church, that alone
was considered worthy of being used in the service
of the gods. It was only the rubric which was allowed to be written in Semitic; the hymns and most
of the prayers were in what had come to be termed
"the pure" or "sacred language" of the Sumerians.
Each hymn is introduced by the words "to be recited," and ends with *amanû*, or "Amen."

The religious services were incessant. Every day
the sacrifice was offered, accompanied by a special
ritual, and the festivals and fasts filled up each
month of the year. There were services even for the
night as well as for the day. The new moons were
strictly observed, and the seventh day was one of
solemn rest. The very name Sabattu or "Sabbath"
was derived by the native etymologists from the
Sumerian words *sa*, "heart," and *bat*, "to end," because it was "a day of rest for the heart." Not only
were there Sabbaths on the seventh, fourteenth,
twenty-first, and twenty-eighth days of the month,
there was also a Sabbath on the nineteenth, that being
the end of the seventh week from the first day of the
previous month. On these Sabbaths no work was
permitted to be done. The King, it was laid down,
" must not eat flesh cooked at the fire or in the smoke;
must not change his clothes; must not put on white
garments; must not offer sacrifices; must not drive
in his chariot; or issue royal decrees." Even the
prophet was forbidden to practise augury or give
medicine to the sick.

From time to time extraordinary days of public humiliation or thanksgiving were ordered to be observed. These were prescribed by the government and were generally the result of some political crisis or danger. When the Assyrian empire, for instance, was attacked by the nations of the north in the early part of Esar-haddon's reign, public prayers and fasts "for one hundred days and one hundred nights" were ordained by the "prophets" in the hope that the Sun-god might "remove the sin" of the people and stave off the threatened attack. So, again, when Assur-bani-pal had suppressed the Babylonian revolt and taken Babylon after a long siege, he tells us that "at the instance of the prophets he purified the mercy-seats and cleansed the processional roads that had been polluted; the wrathful gods and angry goddesses he appeased with special prayers and penitential psalms."

The temple was erected on ground that had been consecrated by libations of wine, oil, and honey, and was a square or rectangular building enclosing an open court, on one side of which was a *ziggurat*, or "tower." The tower was built in successive stages, and in the topmost stage was the shrine of the god. Each "tower" had a name of its own, and was used for astronomical purposes. It corresponded with "the high-place" of Canaan; in the flat plain of Babylonia it was only by means of a tower that the worshipper could "mount up to heaven" and so approach the gods. Herodotus states that the topmost story of the tower attached to the temple of Bel Merodach at Babylon contained nothing but a couch and a table.

The image of the god stood in the innermost shrine or Holy of Holies of the temple itself. In front of it was the golden table on which the shew-bread was laid, and below was the *parakku*, or "mercy-seat," whereon, according to Nebuchadnezzar, at the festival of the new year, "on the eighth and eleventh days, the king of the gods of heaven and earth, Bel, the god, seats himself, while the gods of heaven and earth reverently regard him, standing before him with bowed heads." It was "the seat of the oracles" which were delivered from it by the god to his ministering priests.

In front of the shrine was an altar cased in gold, and another altar stood in the outer court. Here also was the great bason of bronze for purificatory purposes, which was called "the deep," and corresponded with the "sea" of Solomon's temple. Like the latter, it sometimes stood on the heads of twelve bronze oxen, as we learn from a hymn in which the construction of one of these basons is described. They were supposed to represent the primeval "deep" out of which the world has arisen and on which it still floats.

The chapel found by Mr. Hormund Rassam at Balawât, near Nineveh, gives us some idea of what the inner shrine of a temple was like. At its northwest end was an altar approached by steps, while in front of the latter, and near the entrance, was a coffer or ark in which two small slabs of marble were deposited, twelve and one-half inches long by eight wide, on which the Assyrian King Assur-nazir-pal in a duplicate text records his erection of the sanctuary.

It is not surprising that when the Nestorian workmen
found the tablets, they believed that they had discovered the two tables of the Mosaic Law.

The temple sometimes enclosed a Bit-ili or Beth-el.
This was originally an upright stone, consecrated by
oil and believed to be animated by the divine spirit.
The "Black Stone" in the kaaba of the temple of
Mecca is a still surviving example of the veneration
paid by the Semitic nations to sacred stones.
Whether, however, the Beth-els of later Babylonian
days were like the "Black Stone" of Mecca, really
the consecrated stones which had once served as
temples, we do not know; in any case they were
anchored within the walls of the temples which
had taken their place as the seats of the worship
of the gods. Offerings were still made to them
in the age of Nebuchadnezzar and his successors;
thus we hear of 765 "measures" of grain which
were paid as "dues to the Beth-el" by the serfs of
one of the Babylonian temples. The "measure," it
may be stated, was an old measure of capacity, retained among the peasantry, and only approximately
exact. It was calculated to contain from 41 to 43
qas.

The offerings to the gods were divided into sacrifices and meal-offerings. The ox, sheep, lamb, kid,
and dove were offered in sacrifice—fruit, vegetables,
bread, wine, oil, and spices where no blood was
required to be shed. There were also sin-offerings
and heave-offerings, when the offering was first
"lifted up" before the gods. A contract dated in
the thirty-second year of Nebuchadnezzar tells some-

thing about the parts of the animals which were
sacrificed, though unfortunately the meaning of many
of the technical words used in it is still unknown:
" Izkur-Merodach, the son of Imbriya, the son of Ilei-
Merodach, of his own free will has given for the
future to Nebo-balasu-iqbi, the son of Kuddinu, the
son of Ilei-Merodach, the slaughterers of the oxen
and sheep for the sacrifices of the king, the prescribed offerings, the peace-offerings (?) of the whole
year—viz., the caul round the heart, the chine, the
covering of the ribs, the . . . , the mouth of the
stomach, and the . . . , as well as during the year
7,000 sin-offerings and 100 sheep before Iskhara,
who dwells in the temple of Sa-turra in Babylon (not
excepting the soft parts of the flesh, the trotters (?),
the juicy meat, and the salted (?) flesh), and also the
slaughterers of the oxen, sheep, birds, and lambs due
on the 8th day of Nisan, (and) the heave-offering of
an ox and a sheep before Pap-sukal of Bit-Kiduz-
Kani, the temple of Nin-ip and the temple of Anu
on the further bank of the New Town in Babylon."
The 8th of Nisan, or March, was the first day of the
festival of the New Year.

The hierarchy of priests was large. At its head
was the *patesi*, or high-priest, who in the early days
of Babylonian history was a civil as well as an
ecclesiastical ruler. He lost his temporal power with
the rise of the kings. But at first the King was also
a *patesi*, and it is probable that in many cases at
least it was the high-priest who made himself a king
by subjecting to his authority the *patesis* or priestly
rulers of other states. In Assyria the change of the

high-priest into a king was accompanied by revolt
from the supremacy of Babylonia.

With the establishment of a monarchy the high-
priest lost more and more his old power and attributes, and tended to disappear altogether, or to become merely the vicegerent or representative of the
King. The King himself, mindful of his sacerdotal
origin, still claimed semi-priestly powers. But he
now called himself a *sangu* or "chief priest" rather
than a *patesi ;* in fact, the latter name was retained
only from antiquarian motives. The individual high-
priest passed away, and was succeeded by the class
of "chief priests." Under them were several subordinate classes of temple servants. There were, for
instance, the *enû,* or "elders," and the *pasisû,* or
"anointers," whose duty it was to anoint the images
of the gods and the sacred vessels of the temple with
oil, and who are sometimes included among the
ramkû, or "offerers of libations," as well. By the
side of them stood *asipu,* or "prophet," who interpreted the will of heaven, and even accompanied the
army on·its march, deciding when it might attack
the enemy with success, or when the gods refused to
grant it victory. Next to the prophet came the
makhkhû or interpreter of dreams, as well as the
barû, or "seer."

A very important class of temple-servants were the
kalî, or "eunuch-priests," the *galli* of the religions of
Asia Minor. They were under a "chief *kalû,*" and
were sometimes entitled "the servants of Istar." It
was indeed to her worship that they were specially
consecrated, like the *ukhâtu* and *kharimâtu,* or female

hierodules. Erech, with its sanctuary of Anu and Istar, was the place where these latter were chiefly to be found; here they performed their dances in honor of the goddess and mourned over the death of Tammuz.

Closely connected with the *kali* was a sort of monastic institution, which seems to have been attached to some of the Babylonian temples. The *Zikari*, who belonged to it, were forbidden to marry, and it is possible that they were eunuchs like the *kali*. They, too, were under a chief or president, and their main duty was to attend to the daily sacrifice and to minister to the higher order of priests. In this respect they resembled the Levites at Jerusalem; indeed they are frequently termed "servants" in the inscriptions, though they were neither serfs nor slaves. They could be dedicated to the service of the Sun-god from childhood. A parallel to the dedication of Samuel is to be found in a deed dated at Sippara on the 21st of Nisan, in the fifth year of Cambyses, in which "Ummu-dhabat, the daughter of Nebo-bel-uzur," whose father-in-law was the priest of the Sun-god, is stated to have brought her three sons to him, and to have made the following declaration before another priest of the same deity: "My sons have not yet entered the House of the Males (*Zikari*); I have hitherto lived with them; I have grown old with them since they were little, until they have been counted among men." Then she took them into the "House of the Males" and "gave" them to the service of the god. We learn from this and other documents that the *Zikari* lived together

in a monastery or college within the walls of the
temple, and that monthly rations of food were allotted
to them from the temple revenues.

The ordinary priests were married, though the wife
of a priest was not herself a priestess. There were
priestesses, however, as well as female recluses, who,
like the *Zikari*, were not allowed to marry and were
devoted to the service of the Sun-god. They lived in
the temple, but were able to hold property of their
own, and even to carry on business with it. A portion of the profits, nevertheless, went to the treasury
of the temple, out of whose revenues they were themselves supplied with food. From contracts of the
time of Khammurabi we gather that many of them
not only belonged to the leading families of Babylonia, but that they might be relations of the King.

Wholly distinct from these devotees of the Sun-god
were the female hierodules or prostitutes of Istar, to
whom reference has already been made. Distinct
from them, again, were the prophetesses of Istar, who
prophesied the future and interpreted the oracles of
the goddess. One of their chief seats was the temple
of Istar at Arbela, and a collection of the oracles
delivered by them and their brother prophets to Esar-
haddon has been preserved. It is thus that he is
addressed in one of them: "Fear not, O Esar-haddon; the breath of inspiration which speaks to thee
is spoken by me, and I conceal it not. Thine enemies
shall melt away from before thy feet like the floods
in Sivan. I am the mighty mistress, Istar of Arbela,
who have put thine enemies to flight before thy feet.
Where are the words which I speak unto thee, that

thou hast not believed them? I am Istar of Arbela;
thine enemies, the Ukkians, do I give unto thee. I
am Istar of Arbela; in front of thee and at thy side
do I march. Fear not, thou art in the midst of those
that can heal thee; I am in the midst of thy host.
I advance and I stand still!" It is probable that
these prophetesses were not ordained to their office,
but that it depended on their possession of the
"spirit of inspiration." At all events, we find men as
well as women acting as the mouth-pieces of Istar,
and in one instance the woman describes herself as a
native of a neighboring village "in the mountains."

The revenues of the temples and priesthood were
derived partly from endowments, partly from com-
pulsory or voluntary offerings. Among the com-
pulsory offerings were the esrâ, or "tithes." These
had to be paid by all classes of the population from
the King downward, either in grain or in its equivalent in money. The "tithe" of Nabonidos, immediately after his accession, to the temple of the Sun-
god at Sippara was as much as 5 manehs of gold, or
£840. We may infer from this that it was paid on
the amount of cash which he had found in the treasury of the palace and which was regarded as the
private property of the King. Nine years later
Belshazzar, the heir-apparent, offered two oxen and
thirty-two sheep as a voluntary gift to the same
temple, and at the beginning of the following year we
find him paying a shekel and a quarter for a boat to
convey three oxen and twenty-four sheep to the same
sanctuary. Even at the moment when Cyrus was
successfully invading the dominions of his father and

Babylon had already been occupied for three weeks
by the Persian army, Belshazzar was careful to pay
the tithe due from his sister, and amounting to 47
shekels of silver, into the treasury of the Sun-god.
As Sippara was in the hands of the enemy, and
the Babylonian forces which Belshazzar commanded
had been defeated and dispersed, the fact is very
significant, and proves how thoroughly both invaders
and invaded must have recognized the rights of the
priesthood.

Tithe was also indirectly paid by the temple-serfs.
Thus in the first year of Nergal-sharezer, out of 3,100
measures of grain, delivered by "the serfs of the
Sun-god " to his temple at Sippara, 250 were exacted
as "tithe." These serfs must be distinguished from
the temple-slaves. They were attached to the soil,
and could not be separated from it. When, therefore, a piece of land came into the possession of a
temple by gift and endowment, they went along
with it, but their actual persons could not be sold.
The slave, on the other hand, was as much a chattel
as the furniture of the temple, which could be bought
and sold; he was usually a captive taken in war,
more rarely a native who had been sold for debt.
All the menial work of the temple was performed by
him; the cultivation of the temple-lands, on the contrary, was left to the serfs.

It is doubtful whether the "butchers," or slaughterers of the animals required for sacrifice, or the
"bakers " of the sacred cakes, were slaves or freemen.
The expression used in regard to them in the contract of Izkur-Merodach quoted above is open to two

interpretations, but it would naturally signify that they were regarded as slaves. We know, at all events, that many of the artisans employed in weaving curtains for the temples and clothing for the images of the gods belonged to the servile class, and the gorgeousness of the clothing and the frequency with which it was changed must have necessitated a large number of workmen. Many of the documents which have been bequeathed to us by the archives of the temple of the Sun-god at Sippara relate to the robes and head-dresses and other portions of the clothing of the images which stood there.

A considerable part of the property of a temple was in land. Sometimes this was managed by the priests themselves; sometimes its revenues were farmed, usually by a member of the priestly corporation; at other times it was let to wealthy "tenants." One of these, Nebo-sum-yukin by name, who was an official in the temple of Nebo at Borsippa, married his daughter Gigitum to Nergal-sharezer in the first year of the latter's reign.

The state religion of Assyria was a copy of that of Babylonia, with one important exception. The supreme god was the deified state. Assur was not a Baal any more than Yahveh was in Israel or Chemosh in Moab.

He was, consequently, no father of a family, with a wife and a son; he stood alone in jealous isolation, wifeless and childless. It is true that some learned scribe, steeped in Babylonian learning, now and then tried to find a Babylonian goddess with whom to mate him; but the attempt was merely a piece of theological

pedantry which made no impression on the rulers and
people of Nineveh.   Assur was supreme over all
other gods, as his representative, the Assyrian King,
was supreme over the other kings of the earth, and he
would brook no rival at his side.   The tolerance of
Babylonian religion was unknown in Assyria.   It was
"through trust in Assur" that the Assyrian armies
went forth to conquer, and through his help that they
gained their victories.   The enemies of Assyria were
his enemies, and it was to combat and overcome them
that the Assyrian monarchs declare that they marched
to war.   Cyrus tells us that Bel-Merodach was wrathful because the images of other deities had been removed by Nabonidos from their ancient shrines in
order to be gathered together in his temple of Ê-Saggil
at Babylon, but Assur bade his servants go forth
to subdue the gods of other lands, and to compel
their worshippers to transfer their allegiance to the
god of Assyria.   Those who believed not in him
were his enemies, to be extirpated or punished.

It is true that the leading Babylonian divinities
were acknowledged in Assyria by the side of Assur.
But they were subordinate to him, and it is difficult
to resist the impression that their recognition was
mainly confined to the literary classes.   Apart from
the worship of Istar and the use of the names of certain gods in time-honored formulæ, it is doubtful
whether even a knowledge of the Babylonian deities
went much beyond the educated members of the
Assyrian community.   Nebo and Merodach and Anu
were the gods of literature rather than of the popular
cult.

But even in Babylonia the majority of the gods of the state religion was probably but little remembered by the mass of the people. Doubtless the local divinity was well known to the inhabitants of the place over which he presided and where his temple had stood from immemorial times. Every native of Ur was doubtless a devoted adorer of Sin, the Moon-god, and for the inhabitants of Babylon Bel-Merodach was the highest object of worship. But the real religion of the bulk of the population consisted in charms and magic. The Babylonian was intensely superstitious, the cultivated classes as much so as the lowest. Sorcery and divination were not only tolerated by the priests, they formed part of the religious system of the state. Prophets and diviners and interpreters of dreams served in the temples, and one of the sacred books of the priesthood was a collection of incantations and magical rites. Among the people generally the old Shamanistic faith had never been eradicated; it was but partially overlaid with the religious conceptions of the Semite, and sorcery and witchcraft flourished down to the latest days of Babylonian history.

The gods and goddesses were believed to utter oracles and predictions through the lips of inspired men and women. Figures of winged bulls and serpents were placed at the entrance of a building to prevent the demons of evil from passing through it. Before the gates of Babylon Nebuchadnezzar " set up mighty bulls of bronze and serpents which stood erect," and when Nabonidos restored the temple of the Moon-god at Harran two images of the primeval god, Lakhum, were similarly erected on either side of

its eastern gate to "drive back" his "foes." These
protecting genii were known as *sêdi* and *kurubi*, the
shêdim and *cherubim* of the Old Testament. *Sêdi*,
however, was a generic term, including evil as well as
beneficent genii, and the latter was more properly
classed as the *lamassi*, or "colossal forms." The
whole world was imagined to be filled with malevolent spirits ever on the watch to attack and torment
mankind. The water that was drunk, the food that
was eaten, might contain a demon, whom it would be
necessary to exorcise. The diseases that afflict our
bodies, the maladies that prey upon our spirits, were
all due to the spirits of evil, and could be removed
only by the proper incantations and charms. Mad-
ness and epilepsy were more especially the direct
effect of demoniac possession. The magician alone
knew how to cure them; and the priest taught that
his knowledge had first been communicated to him
by the god Ea through his interpreter, Merodach.
Books were written containing the needful formulæ
and ritual for counteracting the malevolence of the
evil spirits and for healing the sick. Pure or "holy"
water and the number seven were regarded as en-
dowed with mysterious power in the performance of
these magical rites; thus magical threads were ordered
to be bound seven times round the limbs of the sick
man, with phylacteries attached to them on which
were inscribed "sentences from a holy book."

It was at night-time that the spirits of evil were
more especially active. It was then that vampires
escaped from the bodies of the dead or from the realm
of Hades to suck the blood of the living, and that the

nightmare lay upon the breast of its victim and sought to strangle him. At the head of these demons of the night was Lilat, the wife of Lil, "the ghost;" from the Babylonians she was borrowed by the Jews, and appears in the book of Isaiah under the name of Lilith.

The demons were served by a priesthood of their own. These were the wizards and witches, and the sorcerers and sorceresses, with whom were associated the public prostitutes, who plied their calling under the shadow of night.

It was then that they lay in ambush for the unwary passenger, for whom they mixed deadly philters which poisoned the blood. They were devotees of Istar, but the Istar they worshipped was a wholly different goddess from the Istar of the official cult. She was a goddess of witchcraft and darkness, of whom it was said that she "seized" on her victim "at night," and was "the slayer of youths." She it was who was dreaded by the people like the witches and "street-walkers," who ministered before her, and against whom exorcisms of all kinds were employed. To guard against her and her agents, small images of Lugal-gira and Allamu, the teraphim of the Babylonians, were made and placed to the right and the left of the door that they might "tear out the hearts of the wicked" and "slay the witch." The Fire-god, moreover, was invoked that he might destroy the ministers of wickedness, and figures of the witch or wizard were moulded in wax and melted in the fire. As the wax dissolved, so, it was prayed, might "the wizard and witch run, melt, and dissolve."

The exorcisms had to be repeated by the victims
of witchcraft. This is clear from the words which
come at the end of each of them : "I, So-and-so, the
son of So-and-so, whose god is So-and-so and goddess So-and-so, I turn to thee, I seek for thee, I kiss
thy hands, I bow myself under thee. Consume the
wizard and the witch ; annihilate the lives of the
sorcerer and the sorceress who have bewitched me.
Then shall I live and gladden thy heart."

In strange contrast to these utterances of popular
superstition are the hymns and prayers that were
addressed by the cultivated Babylonian to the gods of
the official creed. They were gods of light and healing, who punished, indeed, the sins of the wicked,
but were ready to listen to the petitions of the peni-
tent and to forgive them their transgressions. Bel-
Merodach was "the merciful one who raises the dead
to life," and Ea was ever on the watch to send aid
to suffering humanity and foil the demons who
warred against man. Here, for example, are some
extracts from one of those penitential psalms whose
authors seem to have sprung from Eridu and which
formed part of the Babylonian Bible long before the
age of Abraham :

The heart of my lord is wroth ; may it be appeased !
May the god whom I know not be appeased !
May the goddess whom I know not be appeased !
May both the god I know and the god I know not be ap-
    peased ! . . .
O lord, my sins are many, my transgressions are great ! . . .
The sin that I sinned I knew not,
The transgression I committed I knew not. . . .

The lord in the wrath of his heart has regarded me,
God in the fierceness of his heart has revealed himself to
me. . . .
I sought for help, and none took my hand ;
I wept, and none stood at my side ;
I cried aloud, and there was none that heard me.
I am in trouble and hiding ; I dare not look up.
To my god, the merciful one, I turn myself, I utter my
prayer ;
The feet of my goddess I kiss and water with tears. . . .
The sins I have sinned turn into a blessing ;
The transgressions I have committed let the wind carry
away!
Strip off my manifold wickednesses as a garment !
O my god, seven times seven are my transgressions ; for-
give my sins !
O my goddess, seven times seven are my transgressions ; for-
give my sins!

To the same early period belongs a hymn to the
Moon-god, originally composed for the services in
the temple of Ur, the birthplace of Abraham, and
afterward incorporated in the sacred books of the
state religion. It is thus that the poet speaks of his
god :

Father, long-suffering and full of forgiveness, whose hand
upholdeth the life of all mankind ! . . .
First-born, omnipotent, whose heart is immensity, and there
is none who may fathom it ! . . .
In heaven who is supreme? Thou alone, thou art supreme !
On earth, who is supreme? Thou alone, thou art supreme!
As for thee, thy will is made known in heaven, and the an-
gels bow their faces.
As for thee, thy will is made known upon earth, and the
spirits below kiss the ground.

At times the language of the hymn rises to that of
monotheism of a pure and exalted character. That
a monotheistic school actually existed in one of the
literary circles of Babylonia was long ago pointed
out by Sir Henry Rawlinson. It arose at Erech, an
early seat of Semitic influence, and endeavored to
resolve the manifold deities of Chaldea into forms or
manifestations of the "one god," Anu. It never
made many converts, it is true; but the tendency
toward monotheism continued among the educated
part of the population, and when Babylon became
the capital of the country its god, Merodach, became
not only a Bel or "Lord," but the one supreme lord
over all the other gods. Though the existence of the
other gods was admitted, they fell, as it were, into a
background of shadow, and the worshipper of Merodach, in his devotion to the god, almost forgot that
they existed at all. The prayers of Nebuchadnezzar
are a proof how narrow was the line which divided
his faith from that of the monotheist. "To Merodach my lord," he says, "I prayed; I began to him
my petition; the word of my heart sought him, and
I said: O prince, thou that art from everlasting, lord
of all that exists, for the king whom thou lovest,
whom thou callest by name, as it seems good unto
thee, thou guidest his name aright, thou watchest
over him in the path of righteousness! I, the prince
who obeys thee, am the work of thy hands; thou
hast created me and hast entrusted to me the sovereignty over multitudes of men, according to thy
goodness, O lord, which thou hast made to pass over
them all. Let me love thy supreme lordship, let the

fear of thy divinity exist in my heart, and give what seemeth good unto thee, since thou maintainest my life."

The man who could thus pray was not far from the kingdom of God.

APPENDIX

WEIGHTS AND MEASURES

In the preceding pages the equivalence of the *qa* in modern English measures has been given in accordance with the calculations of Dr. Oppert. Other scholars, however, would assign to it a different value, identifying it with the Hebrew *qab* and making it equal to about two litres. This, indeed, seems to have been its value in the age of Abraham, but in the later days of Babylonian history a different system certainly prevailed.

WEIGHTS.

360 se (" grains ")............1 shekel
60 shekels.................1 maneh (*mana*)
60 manehs................ .1 talent

The silver maneh was equivalent to £9, the shekel being 3s., while the gold maneh was ten times its value. The maneh was originally a weight more than one kind of which was in use: (1) The heavy maneh of 990 grammes; (2) the light maneh of 495 grammes; (3) the gold maneh (for weighing gold) of 410 grammes; and (4) the silver maneh of 546 grammes. At Sippara, however, the heavy maneh weighed 787 grammes; the light maneh, 482 grammes; and the gold maneh, 392 grammes; while the standard maneh fixed by Dungi weighed 980 grammes. The maneh of Carchemis contained 561 grammes.

MEASURES OF CAPACITY.

1 *qa* (Heb. *qab*).........................1.66 litres
1 *pi* or ardeb (Heb. homer)............... 36 *qas*
1 *bar* (Heb. se'ah)...................... 60 *qas*
1 homer in Assyria..................... 60 *qas*
1 *gur* (Heb. *kor*) .... 180 *qas*

In the Abrahamic age other systems were in use in Babylonia according to which the *gur* sometimes contained 360 *qas*
and sometimes 300 *qas*.

The tonnage of ships was reckoned by the *gur*.

MEASURES OF LENGTH.

1 *uban* or finger-breadth } 16.6 millimetres
(divided into 180 parts) }
30 finger-breadths ......1 *ammat* or cubit (498 mm.)
2 cubits...............1 great cubit (996 mm.)
6 great cubits.........1 *qanu* or reed
2 reeds................1 *gar*
60 *gars*.................1 *soss* or stade
30 *sosses*...............1 *kasbu* or parasang (21 kilometres)
2 *kasbus*...............1 great *kasbu*

SUPERFICIAL MEASURES.

In the Abrahamic age 180 *se* were probably equivalent to 1
gin, 60 *gin* to one *sar* or "garden," 1,800 *sar* to 1 feddân
(*padânu*) or "acre." The latter was called *bur-gan* in Sumerian, or "10 acres," to distinguish it from a smaller acre,
which contained only 180 *sar*.

Time was reckoned by the *kasbu* or "double hour," and in
early times the weight was divided into three watches of 2
kasbus or 4 hours each. The months were originally lunar,
and consisted of 30 days, an intercalary month being inserted
in the calendar every six years. The zodiac was divided into
360 degrees.

Mathematics were based upon a sexagesimal system, sixty,
called the *soss*, being the unit. The *ner* was equivalent to 10
sosses and the *sar* to 6 *ners*.

INDEX

ADOPTION, by the Sun-god, 36 ; its prevalence in Babylon, 37 : concerning slaves, 38 ff ; a way to citizenship, 41

Ainsworth, on coast-line formation, 2

Allat, goddess of under-world, 242 ; in temples, 247

Amen, used in hymns, 245

Amorites, the, women, 18, 191 ; colonies, 187 ff. ; position of, 189 ; freedom of worship, 191–193 ; country, 220

Apprentices, case of slaves, 71

Arad-Samas, position of his two wives, 27

Aramaic, taught in schools, 56

Architecture, features of Babylonian, 9, 10 ; use of bricks, 90, 137 ; character of, 91 ; plans of houses, 92 ; foundations, 92 ; decorations, 93, 94 ; dwellings of poor, 95 ; staircases, 95

Army. See under "State"

Artists, position of, 166

Ashtoreth. See Istar

Assur, worship of, 256

Assyrians, compared with Babylonians, 8 ; in regard to women, 18 ; slave law among, 78 ; slave contract, 79, 80 ; features of architecture, 93 ; gardens of, 95 ; land, 123 ;

contracts, 124 ; land measurements, 125 ; money interest, 156 ; coinage, 157 ; medicine, 164 ; military character of government, 172 ; taxes, 175 ; army, 181 ; navy, 183 ; letters, 217 ; religion, 255

Astrology, 60 ; letters relating to, 219

BAAL worship, 233–234

Babylonia, its importance and situation, 1 ; the increase of land, 2 ; and its culture, 6 ; various nationalities, 7 ; Chaldean associations, *ibid.* ; Kassite influence, 7, 8 ; the inhabitants, 9 ; trade, *ibid.*, 107 ; architecture, 9 ; writing, 10 ; mode of burial, 10, 11 ; cosmogony, 11 ; fertility, 11, 12 ; features of family life, 13 ff. ; dowry and divorce, 20 ff. ; polygamy, 27 ; matrimony, 29 ; inheritance, 31 ; adoption, 36 ff. ; citizenship, 41 ; names, 45 ff. ; literature, 52 54 ; burial, 62–66 ; slavery, 67 ff. ; labourers, 82 ff., 148 ; manners and customs, 90 ff. ; manufactures, 107 ff. ; house property, 118–120 ; land, 120 ff. ; money - lending, 157 ff. ;

Polygamy, among Babylonians, restricted, 27; but possible, 27, 28
Porcelain, trade in, 137
Portents, the study of, 59, 60
Postal system established, 104; extensive use, 228
Priest, dress of, 101; classes of, 249; eunuch - priests, 250; marriage, 252
Prisons, 206
Professions: bankers, 151; barristers, 161; doctors, 162; poets, 165; musicians, 165, 166; artists, 166
Property, a legal point relating to, 23; a woman's power, *ibid.*; disputes, 42; temple prop, 255
Prostitution in Babylonia, 30, 252
Punishments, legal. *See* "Law"

QUBTÂ, and her slave, 70
Quddâ, and his slave, 70

RAB-MUGI, or court-physician, 164
Rab-saris, office of, 176
Rab-shakeh, or vizier, knowledge of language, 57; office of, 176
Religion, letters relating to, 223; popular superstition, 231, 257; twofold influence in official creed, *ibid.*; Sumerian and Semitic conceptions compared, 232; Shamanism, 235; ideograph, 236; the centres and their influence, 236, 237; Semitic influence, 237 ff.; Istar, 239; Tammuz, 240; the origin of things, 241; various

beliefs, 242; Hades, 242; cosmological, 243; sacred books, 244; hymns, 244, 260; numerous services, 245; temples, 246; sacrifices, 248; hierarchy, 249; temple revenues, 253, 255; witchcraft, 259; exorcisms, 260; monotheism, 263
Rimanni-Bel, a slave's adoption cancelled, 40

SABBATH, origin of word, 245; customs, *ibid.*
Sacred books, 244
Sacrifices, various kinds, 248
Sandals used, 100, 101
Sargon, his empire, 5, 6; a tradition of, 83; houses in time of, 92; dress, 101; survey of land, 122; carpenters' trade under, 134
Satraps, or governors, 176
Schools, 47 ff.; buildings, 54; dead languages taught, 56; subjects of study, 56 ff.
Scribes, the position of, 161
Semites, connection with Sumerians, 4 ff.; influence on religion, 231, 237; Semitic conception of deity, 233; the goddess, 238
Sennacherib's will, 35; garden, 94, 95
Shamanism of the Sumerians, 235
Sheep, largely kept, 109; a contract, 111; duty, *ibid.*; market, 112
Shekel, 158
Ships, character of, 185
Sippara, situation of, 113; letters found at, 214

Printed by BALLANTYNE, HANSON &ᵉ Co.
Edinburgh &ᵉ London